Learn
KQL
in one month

2025 EDITION

Damien Van Robaeys

systanddeploy.com
@syst_and_deploy

Damien VAN ROBAEYS

About the author

My name is Damien Van Robaeys, and I am a French Modern workplace consultant working at Metsys.

I am also a Microsoft MVP for 8 years (published in 2025) in two categories:
- Cloud & Datacenter Management (for PowerShell)
- Enterprise Mobility (for Intune)

I published a lot of articles of my blog, systanddeploy.com, with more than 6 500 000 views.
You can find here a lot of content relative to:
- PowerShell
- Microsoft Intune
- Automation with Intune + PowerShell + Graph API
- Intune reporting with Log Analytics
- Getting started with Log Analytics
- Getting started with Logic Apps

I also wrote two books in French about PowerShell with Jérôme Bezet-Torres:

I am an Official Contributor for the **Modern Endpoint Management** LinkedIn group. This group has for now 42 433 members.
This group is available here below:
https://www.linkedin.com/groups/8761296

In 2023, I created the **Workplace Ninja France** user group and organized it with some awesome guys:
- Jérôme Bezet-Torres
- Mathieu Leroy
- Tom Machado

You can find this user group here below:
- https://www.linkedin.com/company/wpninjasfra
- https://www.workplaceninjas.fr

To follow me, it's here:
- Blog: systanddeploy.com
- X: @syst_and_deploy
- LinkedIn: Damien Van Robaeys
- Mail: damien.vanrobaeys@gmail.com

Don't hesitate to send me a mail if you have a question.
If you have feedback about this book (good or not) don't hesitate to send me a mail ☺ .

About the book

Why this book?

The goal of the book is not to become an expert in KQL after one month but at least to be more comfortable with it and be able to create some cools queries and workbooks.
I always enjoy sharing my knowledge when I learn some new things and that's why I decided to write this book.
I was helping my colleague Abdelkarim to learn KQL by giving him some exercises every day.
After some exercises I thought it could be a cool idea to help more people to learn KQL using this method.
Furthermore, as you may know it's always hard to start learning something new when you're already busy at work, don't have enough time to start learning from scratch or don't have real use case.
Here my goal is to let you learn by yourself but with a bit of structure.
This book is a different approach to learn and I recommend you use also books from Rod Trent to increase your knowledge.

Why the 2025 edition?

The first edition has been published in 2024. Since the publication Microsoft implemented some new features in both Azure and Intune:
- Simple mode in the KQL query editor
- Copilot and KQL
- Intune device query

The 2025 edition will cover them.
I also did some changes to a lot of exercises to use datatable.

Who this book is for?

This book is for people who wants to start with KQL or understand basics of this language by practicing it.
If you are in one of the below cases, this book is for you:
- You heard about KQL but never used it
- You just started with KQL

- You want to use Log Analytics to create dashboard
- You want to use Microsoft Sentinel, Defender XDR...

What will you learn?

In this book, the goal is to start from the basics and go further step by step.
You will first see what KQL is, basics about the Logs explorer, how to use filters, operators, functions, display content from a table, join another table or workspace...
The book is built in a way to progress every day.
Indeed, the name of the book speaks for itself, each day some exercises will be proposed, and you will then find the solution at the end of the book.
Finally, you will also learn how to create a workbook from scratch with a custom lab.

Prerequisites

No specific knowledge is required to read this book but of course you should have basics in IT and know what Microsoft Entra (previously Azure) is, Microsoft Sentinel, Microsoft Defender XDR, Defender for Cloud or other solutions in which you can use KQL.

About exercises in the book

The book is divided in 31 days of exercises but you can manage exercises as you want.
Each day is organized as below:
- Exercises to do on the day
- Key words* to help you with exercises

*Key words to search on the web and helps you finding the solution

On each day you can play with two kinds of environment depending in which domain you work:
- Log Analytics demo environment
- Intune environment

Log Analytics demo environment
The first environment called **Log Analytics demo environment**, is a lab provided by Microsoft giving you access to existing tables and data to start playing with KQL **at no cost**.

The Log Analytics demo env is available here: **aka.ms/LADemo**

When you open it, you have access to many solutions with different logs and data:

▸ LogManagement

▸ Microsoft Sentinel

▸ Network Performance Monitor

▸ Security and Audit

▸ SecurityCenterFree

When you expand solution, you can access to logs as for instance here with the **Security and Audit** and log:

◢ Security and Audit
    ▸ ⊞ ProtectionStatus
    ▸ ⊞ SecurityBaseline
    ▸ ⊞ SecurityBaselineSummary

In many exercises, we will create our own data lab with fake data using the **datatable** operator. This one allows us to create a table with fake data that we can use in our exercises.
See below an overview:

```
let Devices=datatable
(username:string,device:string,manufacturer:string,model:str
ing,SN:string)
[
        "luca","LENO_TST2","lenovo","T14s","",
        "damien","LENO_TST3","lenovo","T14s","TERY67",
        "angel","TEST","dell","XPS 15","U8INYN",
        "mattias","DELL1","Dell","XPS 13",""
];
```

This will create a table containing fake data, as below, with which we can play.

	username	device	manufacturer	model	SN
>	luca	LENO_TST2	lenovo	T14s	
>	damien	LENO_TST3	lenovo	T14s	TERY67
>	angel	TEST	dell	XPS 15	U8INYN
>	mattias	DELL1	Dell	XPS 13	

We will also load data directly from an external source, from JSON files on my GitHub:
- Devices.json
- BSOD.json
- BIOS_Lab.json

See below an overview of what contain each files:

- **Devices.json**

```
[
    {
        "devicename": "Computer1",
        "username": "damien.vanrobaeys",
        "manufacturer": "lenovo"
    },
    {
        "devicename": "Computer2",
        "username": "luca.vanrobaeys",
        "manufacturer": "lenovo"
    },
```

- **BSOD.json**

```
{
    "devicename": "Computer1",
    "BSODCount": "4",
    "BSODCode": "0x000000A0",
    "Model": "ThinkPad T480s",
    "BIOSVersion": "1.49"
},
```

- **BIOS_Lab.json**

```
{
    "ComputerName": "LP00001",
    "UserName": "Damien",
    "DeviceModel": "T14s",
    "NotUpdatedSince": "0",
    "CurrentVersionBIOS": "1.21",
    "NewVersionBIOS": "1.21",
    "BIOSStatus": "uptodate",
    "ScriptStatus": "Success",
    "DateDiffDelay": "0"
},
```

Intune environment

If you work with Intune every day, I recommend playing with this environment after playing with the demo lab.

A prerequisite is to send Intune data to your Log Analytics workspace, you can do this by following below instructions: https://www.systanddeploy.com/2022/08/starting-with-log-analytics-part-4.html

You can access to the Intune logs by proceeding as below:
- Go to your Log Analytics workspace
- Go to **Logs**
- Go to **LogManagement**

Favorites

You can add favorites the ☆ icon

▸ AzureResources

◢ LogManagement

- There you will find Intune Logs

    ▸ ⊞ IntuneAuditLogs

    ▸ ⊞ IntuneDeviceComplianceOrg

    ▸ ⊞ IntuneDevices

Learn more about KQL!

In this part you will find interesting resources to get deeper knowledge about KQL.

Website and links

- **KQL Cheat sheets**
https://techcommunity.microsoft.com/t5/azure-data-explorer-blog/azure-data-explorer-kql-cheat-sheets/ba-p/1057404

- **KQL quick reference**
https://learn.microsoft.com/en-us/azure/data-explorer/kusto/query/kql-quick-reference

- **KQL best practices**
https://learn.microsoft.com/en-us/azure/data-explorer/kusto/query/best-practices

- **KQL Search**
https://www.kqlsearch.com

- **Must learn KQL series**
https://github.com/rod-trent/MustLearnKQL

- **ArcaneCode**
https://arcanecode.com/category/kql/

- **KustoKing**
https://www.kustoking.com

- **KQL Query**
https://kqlquery.com

- **KQL LinkedIn page**
https://www.linkedin.com/company/kql

Books

- **Must learn KQL**
  - ✓ Author: Rod Trent
  - ✓ Link: https://www.amazon.com/Must-Learn-KQL-Essential-Cloud-focused/dp/B0B1C9Y3TK

- **The definitive guide to KQL**
  - ✓ Authors: Rod Trent, Mark Morowczynski, Matthew Luke Zorich
  - ✓ Link: https://www.amazon.com/Must-Learn-KQL-Essential-Cloud-focused/dp/B0B1C9Y3TK

- **KQL: a gateway to Microsoft Sentinel**
  - ✓ Author: Samik Roy
  - ✓ Link: https://a.co/d/fV97AP4

People to follow on Twitter/X

- Rod Trent (@rodtrent)
- Kijo Girardi (@kj_ninja25)
- Ugur koc (@UgurKocDe)
- KQL Cafe (@KqlCafe)
- Bert Jan (@BertJanCyber)

People to follow on LinkedIn

- Rod Trent
- Tzvia Gitlin Troyna
- Ugur Koc
- Kijo Girardi
- Steven Lim

Back to basics

What is KQL?

Kusto Query Language aka **KQL** is a request language used to write queries to explore data/content of Logs and tables.
It's a powerful tool and language allowing you to query content of a log to get result and share it through a dashboard or export it for instance to a file format.
Structure of KQL is like SQL, you can find things like tables, columns, rows of data, database and you can join different tables between each other by using a common id.

Where is it used?

KQL is used in a lot of Microsoft solution:
- Log Analytics/Azure Monitor
- Azure Data Explorer
- Microsoft Sentinel
- M365 Defender
- Device query part from Intune

It's a language used a lot in Cyber Security and threat hunting stuff.
You can use for instance KQL to check which process are running on devices, which registry keys have been created or modified, on which websites users have been navigating...
If you want to work in Security job, KQL is essential.

Why KQL?

KQL is the acronym of Kusto Query Language but why this name of Kusto?
Even if it's not official, Kusto if for the well-known French undersea pioneer, **Jacques Cousteau (Kusto)**. Indeed, you can find on the KQL Microsoft docs some references about Jacques Cousteau.

For instance, on the below page, you can find some information about him:
https://learn.microsoft.com/en-au/azure/data-explorer/kusto/query/datatableoperator?pivots=azuremonitor

---

```
datatable(Date:datetime, Event:string, MoreData:dynamic) [
    datetime(1910-06-11), "Born", dynamic({"key1":"value1", "key2":"value
    datetime(1930-01-01), "Enters Ecole Navale", dynamic({"key1":"value3"
    datetime(1953-01-01), "Published first book", dynamic({"key1":"value5
    datetime(1997-06-25), "Died", dynamic({"key1":"value7", "key2":"value
]
| where strlen(Event) > 4
| extend key2 = MoreData.key2
```

See below references on Wikipedia:

Born	Jacques-Yves Cousteau
	11 June 1910
	Saint-André-de-Cubzac, Gironde, France
Died	25 June 1997 (aged 87)
	Paris, France

Log structure

KQL is used to explore data from Logs.
As with SQL, data are located into tables and organized into columns and rows of data.

To have a first overview of KQL let's go to the Log Analytics demo environment (link mentioned previously).
We will open the **SigninLogs** log as below:
1. Expand the **LogManagement** solution
2. Go to **SigninLogs**

Now let's expand the **SigninLogs** to see its structure:

⊿ ⊞ SigninLogs

    t AADTenantId (string)

    t AlternateSignInName (string)

    t AppDisplayName (string)

    t AppId (string)

You can see that this Log/Table contains different fields/columns with different type (here string).
KQL supports the following types: boolean, integer, real, decimal, dates, timespan, string, GUID, dynamic (JSON)

First overview

Here below is the query editor that you can find in different solutions like Log Analytics or Microsoft Defender:

On the left side, you can find different items available:

🏷 Tables

🗃 Queries

{ƒ} Functions

🕓 Query history

See below what does each item:

- Tables: list of logs/custom logs available in your workspace
- Queries: KQL queries you have saved
- Function: functions you have saved
- Query history: KQL queries that have been executed

Tables are organized in different solutions like LogManagement, Update Compliance, Custom Logs...

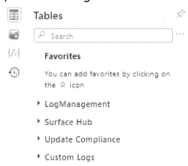

On the upper right side, you can find the query editor zone.

Select a table   Time range: Last 24 hours   Limit 1000   Run   Simple mode ∨

On the upper left side, two modes are available:
- Simple mode: provide easy way to start with KQL
- KQL mode: provide advanced way to play with KQL

See below what Microsoft says about both modes:

KQL is a powerful, easy to learn query language, however, as any query language it requires some knowledge to operate.

Simple mode experience was created to bridge this knowledge gap - allowing most popular KQL operators and actions to be utilized using a very simple, point-and-click experience requiring no KQL knowledge at all!

KQL Mode gives advanced users the full power of Kusto Query Language (KQL) to derive deeper insights from their logs.

Simple mode

The first step to start with this mode is to select a table.
1. Click on **Select a table**

 Select a table

2. Select your table (here IntuneDevices from LogManagement)
3. Content from your table will be displayed with all columns.

When you are in this mode, a Add filter is available (we will see it just after).

KQL mode

This mode is the "advanced mode" and it lets you play with your data by typing your own KQL queries by yourself.
Type you query in the blank space then click on the **Run** blue button to run the query and display results.
Now let's double-click on the SigninLogs mentioned previously to run our first query and display content from this log.

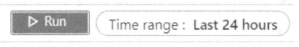

```
1   SigninLogs
```

Results will be displayed in the **Results** part below:

TimeGenerated [UTC]	ResourceId	OperationName	OperationVersion
> 12/27/2023, 3:07:43.145 PM	/tenants/4b2462a4-bbee-495a-a0e1-f23ae524cc9c/provide...	Sign-in activity	1.0
> 12/27/2023, 3:37:17.453 PM	/tenants/4b2462a4-bbee-495a-a0e1-f23ae524cc9c/provide...	Sign-in activity	1.0
> 12/27/2023, 3:37:17.453 PM	/tenants/4b2462a4-bbee-495a-a0e1-f23ae524cc9c/provide...	Sign-in activity	1.0
> 12/27/2023, 3:41:13.877 PM	/tenants/4b2462a4-bbee-495a-a0e1-f23ae524cc9c/provide...	Sign-in activity	1.0
> 12/27/2023, 3:13:51.350 PM	/tenants/4b2462a4-bbee-495a-a0e1-f23ae524cc9c/provide...	Sign-in activity	1.0
> 12/27/2023, 3:14:57.641 PM	/tenants/4b2462a4-bbee-495a-a0e1-f23ae524cc9c/provide...	Sign-in activity	1.0
> 12/27/2023, 3:17:13.201 PM	/tenants/4b2462a4-bbee-495a-a0e1-f23ae524cc9c/provide...	Sign-in activity	1.0
> 12/27/2023, 2:45:24.646 PM	/tenants/4b2462a4-bbee-495a-a0e1-f23ae524cc9c/provide...	Sign-in activity	1.0

You can then see the structure of the Log with all columns displayed and rows of data, one row for each entry.

Limit and Add

The **Limit** operator is available in both Simple and KQL modes.

Time range : Last 24 hours   Limit : **1000**

It allows you to filter/configure the number of entries to display in the result pane.

The default limit is 1000.

This one can be configured in your KQL queries by adding limit operator as below:

```
| limit 500
```

The **Add** button is available is available only in the Simple mode. This one allows you to add operators and configure your query by using user friendly mode.
It looks like as below by default:

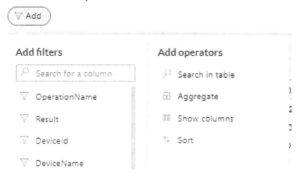

Using **Add filters**, you can filter on a specific entry.

In the below example we want to filter on a specific Device name:
1. In **Add filters**, click on **DeviceName**
2. Select operator **Equals**
3. Type the name of the device

In the below example we want to show result where device name starts with a specific string:
1. In **Add filters**, click on **DeviceName**
2. Select operator **Starts with**
3. Type the string you want to search like desktop

You can add multiple filters to your query using the **Add** button.

Time range vs TimeGenerated

One important thing to notice with KQL is that you need to specify a time range to define the period of the activity you want to show.
Here by default the time range is configured to last 24 hours.

Time range : Last 24 hours

Here we run a query on the SigninLogs with time range 24 hours meaning I want to display all records from the Log during the last 24 hours (with an activity during the last day).
In each log/table you will find a column called **TimeGenerated** (date type) corresponding to the time of the record activity.
All log tables within Azure Monitor Logs are required to have a **TimeGenerated** column populated with the timestamp of the logged event.

Save, Share, Export

Save your query to save your time
The query editor has different useful buttons that can save your time.
Let's imagine we have built a cool query that you can use often. You don't want to type it again and again and again...
First because it's boring and secondly because you want to avoid any human typing mistakes.
After executing your query, just click on the **Save** button then **Save as query**.

This will save your query to reuse it whenever you want by just running it again.

Share or Export with the world

With the world or at least with your colleagues ☺

This option allows you as you can see below, to share your query with someone else.

Export query results

This button can help you a lot in some case. For instance, you must run a specific query to check some security stuff on enrolled devices and you must share results with your manager and colleagues. Instead of sharing them the query and let them execute it, why not execute the query and export result to a file. This is the goal of this button.

After clicking on it, you will see different options:

- Export to CSV all columns or just displayed
- Open in Excel
- Export to PBI

The PBI export can be useful if you're more comfortable with Power BI for reporting stuff. Indeed, it allows you to export your KQL query to a M query format that you can use in a Power BI dashboard.

KQL basics

Here we will learn some basics of KQL before starting with the exercises.

Commenting a line

Commenting a line allows you to exclude this one from the query execution meaning it won't be interpreted.
In PowerShell or other languages, comment is useful to explain what a code or lines do.
Whereas in PowerShell the comment character is #, with KQL the comment character is **//**.
Here below I have commented this line: Hello world, let's learn KQL together.
`// Hello world, let's learn KQL together`

Note: Later in the book, we will see how to add a comment easily with a shortcut combination.

Pipe: the key to a query

As mentioned previously KQL is used to play with data from logs/tables. With KQL there are some syntaxes to follow.
The first one is to use the pipe "|" character.
In KQL each operation on a log is delineated by a pipe and executed in the same order they have been written.
The pipe character allows you to add filters to your query and get the result you need.
Each time you want to add an operator or function you will need to add a pipe "|".

where: wherever you will go

The other key of KQL is **where** operator. Both the **pipe** and **where** are essentials to write good queries.
The **where** operator allows you to match on a condition and limit result of your query.

For instance, you have a list of all devices, in the log IntuneDevices, and you want to filter the result only on a specific device with a specific name.

To proceed, just use both pipe and where operator as below:

`IntuneDevices | where <your condition>`

Then next step is to specify the condition meaning the column on which we want to filter the result, here column Devicename, as below:

`IntuneDevices | where Devicename=="Name of the device"`

Note here the double "=", we will see this later in details

where operator does not work alone, you need to add some other operators to specify conditions you want to match.

See below different operators to use with Where and a specific value or string:

Operator	Meaning	Case-sentivive
==	Equals	Yes
=~	Equals	No
!=	Not equals	Yes
!~	Not equals	No
<>	Not equals	No
Contains	Contains	No
Contains_cs	Contains	Yes
!contains	Not contains	No
!contains_cs	Not contains	Yes
Startswith	Starts with	No
startswith_cs	Starts with	Yes
Endswith	Ends with	No
endswith_cs	Ends with	Yes

See below those operators in action:

Operator test	Result
"aBc"=="aBc"	True
"aBc"=="abc"	False
"aBc"!="abc"	True
"aBc"!="aBc"	False

"aBc"~="abc"	True
"hello" contains "he"	True
"hello" contains "lo"	True
"hello" contains "abc"	false
"paris" startswith "pa"	True
"paris" startwith "abc"	false
"paris" endswith "ris"	True

See below different operators to use with Where and a list of strings:

Operator	Meaning
Has	Equals
!has	Not equals
In	In a list of elements
!in	Not in a list of elements

See below those operators in action:

Operator test	Result
"psg" in ("abc","psg","cba")	True
"ABC" in ("abc","psg","cba")	False

project: choosing what to display

By default, when you query a log, all columns will be displayed. It can take some resources and can be a bit unreadable in a report.
That's why it can be useful to choose which columns to display in your report.
For this the operator to use is **project**.
In the below example we want to show columns DeviceName, LastContact and Model from the IntuneDevices log:

```
IntuneDevices | project DeviceName, LastContact, Model
```

See below some variants of the project operator:

Operator	Meaning
| project	Choose columns to display
| project-away	Remove a specific column
| project-reorder	Reorder columns display
| project-keep	Keep the column
| project-rename	Rename a column

Useful Keyboard shortcut

With KQL, you can use keyboard shortcut to make your task easy.

See below some useful shortcuts that you can use in the query editor:

Shortcut	Description
Ctrl+K+C	Add a comment
Ctrl+K+U	Remove a comment
Ctrl+Enter	Add pipe and go to new line
Ctrl+Z	Undo
Ctrl+Y	Redo
Ctrl+H	Open replace dialog
Ctrl+F	Open search dialog
Ctrl+G	Go to specific line

KQL and Copilot

Unless you have been alone on an island or completely disconnected from the world, you have probably heard about Copilot, because Copilot is now almost everywhere.

With the help of Copilot, you can now create/generate your KQL queries to play with your data and create the perfect dashboard.

How to use it?

In the Azure portal, you can find a Copilot button just after the search bar.

When you click on it, a left pane will be opened.
Type what you need here below:

Now you just type your request in the search bar.
It will generate your KQL query with some explanations.

KQL & Copilot in action

Let's take exercises from the day 6.
We first want to get the following information: In the SigninLogs, display all records where the column UserType equals Member.

We will now ask Copilot to create the KQL query:

create a KQL query to display records from the table Perf.
Create a new column FreeSizeGB and convert CounterValue
to GB

See below the result:

create a KQL query to display records from the table
SigninLogs where the column UserType equals Member

```
SigninLogs
| where UserType == "Member"
```

This KQL query filters the SigninLogs table to display
records where the UserType column equals
"Member".

Now let's take the example from the day 7.
See below the result:

create a KQL query to display records from the table Perf.
Create a new column FreeSizeGB and convert CounterValue
to GB

```
Perf
| extend FreeSizeGB = CounterValue / 1024
| project FreeSizeGB, *
```

This KQL query filters the Perf table and creates a
new column FreeSizeGB by converting the
CounterValue to GB. It then projects the new column
along with all other columns.

In the following example, we want to generate a KQL query to
join two tables Table1 and Table2.

See below the result:

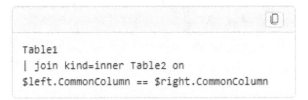

Generate a KQL query to join two tables in Log Analytics.

To join two tables in Log Analytics using KQL, you can use the join operator. Here is an example query:

```
Table1
| join kind=inner Table2 on
$left.CommonColumn == $right.CommonColumn
```

Replace Table1 and Table2 with the names of the tables you want to join, and CommonColumn with the name of the column that both tables have in common.

Intune device query

The device query is probably one of the most excited features in Intune.
One of the big challenges with Intune (and the cloud world) is to get on real time information about devices.
The device query is now here for that.
See below more information:
https://learn.microsoft.com/en-us/mem/analytics/device-query

Prerequisite

See below recommendation from Microsoft about prerequisites:

To use Device query in your tenant, you must have a license that includes Microsoft Intune Advanced Analytics. Advanced Analytics features are available with:

- *The Intune Advanced Analytics Add-on*
- *Microsoft Intune Suite*

To use Device query on a device, the device must be enrolled in Endpoint Analytics. Learn how to enroll a device in Endpoint Analytics.

For a user to use Device query, you must assign the Managed Devices - Query permission to them.

To use Device query, devices must be Intune managed and corporate owned.

Device query structure

To access to the device query, the first step is to select a device. You can find the Device query here below:

Remediations (preview)

Device query

The device query is organized in two parts:

On the left side, all properties that can be accessed are listed. See below properties available with device query:

- BiosInfo
- Certificate
- Cpu
- DiskDrive
- EncryptableVolume
- FileInfo
- LocalGroup
- LocalUserAccount
- LogicalDrive
- MemoryInfo
- OsVersion
- Process
- SystemEnclosure
- SystemInfo
- Tpm
- WindowsAppCrashEvent
- WindowsDriver
- WindowsEvent
- WindowsQfe
- WindowsRegistry
- WindowsService

You can see structure of a property by extending it. For instance, click on **BiosInfo** to see its structure:

∧ BiosInfo

Manufacturer

ReleaseDateTi...

SerialNumber

SmBiosVersion

It means that you can get the above information by running this query.

On the right side, you can find the KQL query zone, where to type your queries.

Intune device query and KQL

Now let's have a look of the KQL side with device query by exploring different properties.

Exploring the registry
The registry is a huge place to get plenty of information about the device, applications and a lot of things that are running on the device.
See below how to get registry info with KQL and the device query feature:

```
WindowsRegistry('Registry path)
```

In the below example we want to get information about application 7-Zip on a device.

See below the registry path where to find it:
HKEY_LOCAL_MACHINE\SOFTWARE\Microsoft\Windows\CurrentVersion\Uninstall\7-Zip

The KQL query is the following one:

```
WindowsRegistry('HKEY_LOCAL_MACHINE\SOFTWARE\Microsoft\Windows\CurrentVersion\Uninstall\7-Zip')
```

See below the result:

RegistryKey	ValueName	ValueType	ValueData
HKEY_LOCAL_MAC...	DisplayName	REG_SZ	7-Zip 24.08 (x64)
HKEY_LOCAL_MAC...	DisplayVersion	REG_SZ	24.08
HKEY_LOCAL_MAC...	DisplayIcon	REG_SZ	C:\Program Files\7-Zip\7zFM.exe

By default, all columns are displayed.

∧ WindowsRegistry

RegistryKey

ValueData

ValueName

ValueType

Now we just want to show the **displayversion** value. For that, we will use **where** operator as below:

```
WindowsRegistry('HKEY_LOCAL_MACHINE\SOFTWARE\Microsoft\Windows\CurrentVersion\Uninstall\7-Zip')
| where ValueName=="DisplayVersion"
```

See below the result:

▷ Run ✕ Clear input ⋯

```
1 WindowsRegistry('HKEY_LOCAL_MACHINE\SOFTWARE\Microsoft\Windows\CurrentVersion\Uninstall\7-Zip')
2 | where ValueName=="DisplayVersion"
```

Get started   Results

☰ Columns ∨

RegistryKey	ValueName	ValueType	ValueData
HKEY_LOCAL_MAC...	DisplayVersion	REG_SZ	24.08

To only displaying the version, we will use the **project** operator:

```
WindowsRegistry('HKEY_LOCAL_MACHINE\SOFTWARE\Microsoft\Windo
ws\CurrentVersion\Uninstall\7-Zip')
| where ValueName=="DisplayVersion"
| project ValueData
```

Getting BIOS information

In the following example, we need to get information about current BIOS on the device, version, and release date.

The KQL query is the following one:

```
BiosInfo
| project SmBiosVersion, ReleaseDateTime
```

See below the result:

Get started   Results

▤ Columns ∨

SmBiosVersion	ReleaseDateTime
N2YET40W (1.29)	2023-11-21T00:00:00Z

Exercises summary

See below KQL things you will learn day by day:

- Day 1: Log display (project-reorder, away, getschema, type)
- Day 2: Columns & time range (project, timegenerated, ago)
- Day 3: Renaming columns (project, project-rename)
- Day 4: Limit records (limit, take, arg_max)
- Day 5: Search string in tables (search, where, in, distinct)
- Day 6: Filtering (has, has_all, has_any, contains, ==, in)
- Day 7: Filtering part 2 (not, startswith, isnotempty)
- Day 8: Create custom columns (extend, where, in)
- Day 9: Sort & order records (order, sort, top)
- Day 10: Records counting (summarize, count, countif)
- Day 11: Condition if, then, else (iif, extend)
- Day 12: Create variable (let, print)
- Day 13: Date time (make_datetime, datetime_add, timezone)
- Day 14: Date time part 2 (format_datetime, datetime_diff)
- Day 15: Date interval (ago, between, make_datetime)
- Day 16: Records parsing (parse)
- Day 17: Records parsing part 2 (parse_json, parse_xml)
- Day 18: Playing with version (parse_version, extend)
- Day 19: Playing with strings (split, let, strcat, substring)
- Day 20: Case condition (case)
- Day 21: Replace strings (replace, replace_strings, dynamic)
- Day 22: Records counting part 2 (count, summarize, case)
- Day 23: Create data table (datatable)
- Day 24: Join tables part 1 (join, project-away)
- Day 25: Join tables part 2 (inner, kind, join)
- Day 26: Join tables part 3
- Day 27: Join tables part 4 (union, lookup)
- Day 28: Play with different workspace data (workspace, join)
- Day 29: Play with external data (externaldata)
- Day 30: Join external data (externaldata, join)
- Day 31: More actions (encode/decode base64, locate ip...)
- Bonus: create a workbook lab

EXERCISES

 # DAY 1

Exercises of the day

Intune environment

1. Display records from the IntuneDevices log
2. Change columns order by displaying LastContact first
3. Hide following columns: OperationName, Result, GraphDeviceIsManaged, Type
4. Show schema of the log (meaning columns type)
5. Get type of the LastContact column with KQL then portal
6. Get type of following values: a, 111, 1=1, now(), 1s

Demo lab environment

1. Open aka.ms/LADemo
2. Display records from the SecurityEvent log
3. Change columns order by displaying Activity first
4. Hide following columns: EventSourceName, Channel, AdditionalInfo, AdditionalInfo2, AuthenticationPackageName
5. Show schema of the log (meaning columns type)
6. Get type of the Channel column with KQL then portal
7. Get type of following values: a, 111, 1=1, now(), 1s

Q Key words

- project, reorder, away
- gettype(), getschema, ColumnName

 DAY 2

🗒 Exercises of the day

Intune environment

1. In the IntuneDevices log, display only the following columns: TimeGenerated, LastContact, DeviceName, Model, SerialNumber,UserName,upn
2. Display results from the last hour
   - From the query editor
   - Directly in your query
3. Display results from the last 7 days
   - From the query editor
   - Directly in your query

Demo lab environment

1. Open aka.ms/LADemo
2. In the SecurityEvent log, display only the following columns: TimeGenerated, Account, Computer, EventID, Activity
3. Display results from the last hour
   - From the query editor
   - Directly in your query
4. Display results from the last 7 days
   - From the query editor
   - Directly in your query

🔍 Key words

- project
- timegenerated, time range, ago
- summarize, arg_max, by

 DAY 3

Exercises of the day

Demo lab environment

1. Open aka.ms/LADemo
2. Use the below datatable

```
let Devices=datatable
(username:string,device:string,serialnumber:string,model:string)
[
"luca","DEVICE1","E3QTSY","T14s Gen1",
"damien","DEVICE2","AZJTOL","T14s"
];
```

3. Rename columns as below:
    - username: user
    - devicename: device
    - SerialNumber: SN
4. Rename columns by adding blank space as below:
    - username: user name
    - devicename: device name
    - serialumber: serial number
    - model: model

🔍 Key words

- project, rename
- ['']

 DAY 4

 **Exercises of the day**

Intune environment

1. In the IntuneDevices log, filter on device name by clicking on the DeviceName column header
2. There are many records for the same device. Why?
3. On the last 7 days, keep only the last result for each device
4. Display 10 records randomly

Demo lab environment

1. Open aka.ms/LADemo
2. In the SecurityEvent log, filter on the device name by clicking on the Account column header
3. There are many records for the same device, why?
4. On the last 7 days, keep only the last result for each account
5. Display 10 records randomly

Q **Key words**

- timegenerated, summarize, by
- take

DAY 5

Exercises of the day

1. Open aka.ms/LADemo
2. Use the below datatable
```
let Devices=datatable
(username:string,device:string,manufacturer:string,model:string)
[
"luca","DEVICE1","LENOVO","T14s Gen1",
"damien","DEVICE2","lenovo","T14s",
"stephen","TEST2","Lenovo","T14s Gen 3",
"stephen","TEST2","Lenovo","T14s Gen 3",
"christophe","TEST3","lenovo","T14s gen4",
"evrard","TEST3","lenovo","T14s Gen2",
"myriam","DKTP-123","lenovo","T14S Gen2",
];
```
3. Search everything containing word "luca"
4. Do the same with word "LENOVO" or "lenovo"
5. What did you notice?
6. Make the research case sensitive
7. Add the below datatable
```
let Devices2=datatable
(username:string,device:string,manufacturer:string,model:string)
[
"luca","DEVICE1","LENOVO","T14s Gen1",
"angel","DEVICE3","dell","XPS 15",
"abdelkarim","LPTP-321","dell","XPS 13"
];
```
8. Search for the word "luca" in both tables Devices & Devices2
9. In the Devices table remove duplicated rows

Q Key words

- search, in
- distinct

 DAY 6

Exercises of the day

1. Open aka.ms/LADemo
2. Use the below query to create a Devices datatable

```
let Devices=datatable (data:string)
[
'{"username": "damien","device": "LENO_TST1","manufacturer":
"lenovo","model":"T480s","SN":"TR6EYN"}',
'{"username": "luca","device": "LENO_TST3","manufacturer":
"LENOVO","model":"T14s","SN":"TERY67"}',
'{"username": "angel","device": "TEST","manufacturer":
"dell","model":"XPS 15","SN":"U8INYN"}',
'{"username": "mattias","device": "DELL1","manufacturer":
"Dell","model":"XPS 13","SN":""}'
];
```

3. Display records with word "lenovo" using has
4. Display records with word "LENOVO" using has
5. What did you notice?
6. Display records with word "lenovo" or "dell" using has_any
7. Display records with word "lenovo" and "luca" using has_all
8. Display records with word "lenovo" using contains
9. Display records with word "LENOVO" using contains
10. What did you notice?
11. Display records with word "lenovo" or "dell" using contains
12. Display records with word "lenovo" and "luca" using contains
13. What did you notice between has and contains?
14. Display records with word "lenovo" using "=="
15. What did you notice?
16. Use the below query to create a new table with fake data

```
let Devices=datatable
(username:string,device:string,manufacturer:string,model:string,SN:
string)
[
        "luca","LENO_TST2","Lenovo","T14s","",
        "kevin","LENO_TST3","lenovo","T14s","TERY67",
        "angel","TEST","dell","XPS 15","U8INYN",
        "mattias","DELL1","Dell","XPS 13",""];
```

17. Display records where manufacturer is Lenovo with "=="
18. Do the same with manufacturer is "Lenovo"
19. What did you notice?
20. Display records where Manufacturer is "lenovo" or "LENOVO" using contains
21. Make it case-sensitive using contains
22. Display records where manufacturer contains "leno" using contains
23. Display records where manufacturer is "Lenovo" using has
24. Display records where manufacturer is "dell" or "Lenovo" using has_any
25. Display records where manufacturer is "lenovo" using the in operator
26. Display records where manufacturer is "LENOVO" using the in operator
27. What did you notice?
28. Make it case insensitive
29. Display records where manufacturer is "lenovo" or "dell" using the in operator
30. Display records where manufacturer contains "novo" using in and has operator
31. What did you notice?

Q Key words

- has, contains, contains_cs
- equals, where, in

DAY 7

📊 Exercises of the day

1. Open aka.ms/LADemo
2. Use the query 1, from the previous day
3. Display records not containing "lenovo" (not)
4. Display records not containing "dell" or "lenovo" (not)
5. Display records not containing "damien" and "lenovo" (not)
6. Display records not containing "lenovo" (has or contains)
7. Use the query 15, from the previous day
8. Display records where manufacturer is not Lenovo (not, !contains, !has, !equals, !in)
9. Display records where devicename starts with "leno"
10. Display records where SN is not empty
11. Display records where SN is empty
12. Display records where SN and username are not empty

Key words

- where, has, contains, equals, in
- !has, !contains, !=, !in, not
- isempty, isnotempty

DAY 8

👨‍🏫 Exercises of the day

Demo lab environment

1. Open aka.ms/LADemo
2. Use the following datatable
```
let Devices=datatable
(username:string,device:string,StorageFree:long,StorageTotal:long)
[
        "luca","DEVICE1","30494","242196",
        "damien","DEVICE2","119382","242533",
        "angel","DEVICE3","187654","242533",
        "mattias","DESKTOP6-RRT","50352","242165",
        "nicklas","TEST1","21038","242181",
        "stephen","TEST2","29123","242921",
        "franck","MYCOMP","196123","242533",
        "christophe","HELLOWORLD","7859","242551",
        "jax","SAMCRO","149965","241921"
];
```
3. Add two columns StorageTotalGB, StorageFreeGB with previous size converted to GB
4. Calculate the used size on disk in a new column UsedSize
5. Convert UsedSize to GB
6. Add a column FreePercent with the free disk size percentage

Intune environment

1. In IntuneDevices log, keep last record for all devices
2. Do the same than in "demo lab env" part 2, 3, 4, 5

🔍 Key words

- where, in, extend, arg_max, timegenerated

 # DAY 9

Exercises of the day

Demo lab environment

1. Open aka.ms/LADemo
2. Use the previous query to get FreePercent
3. Sort result on the device name
4. Sort result on the free disk space percentage
5. Display randomly 5 devices where free disk space percentage is lesser than 50%
6. Display top 5 devices with most free disk space percentage

Intune environment

1. Use the IntuneDevices log
2. Do the same than in "demo lab env" part 2, 3, 4, 5, 6

Q Key words

- sort, order
- top

DAY 10

Exercises of the day

Demo lab environment

1. Open aka.ms/LADemo
2. Use the previous query to get free disk percent
3. Display records where free disk percent is lesser than 20%
4. Display records count
5. Display devices count where free disk percent is lesser than or equals to 5%
6. Display devices count where free disk percent is between 20% and 50%
7. Create different column as below:
   - Less 5%
   - Between 5% and 20%
   - Between 20% and 50%
   - Above 60%: percent > 60%

Intune environment

1. Use the IntuneDevices log
2. Use the previous query to get free disk percent
3. Do the same than in "demo lab env" part 2, 3, 4, 5, 6, 7

🔍 Key words

- summarize
- count, countif

 DAY 11

Exercises of the day

Demo lab environment

1. Open aka.ms/LADemo
2. Use the following datatable

```
let Devices=datatable
(username:string,device:string,StorageFree:long,StorageTotal:long,A
ction:string)
[
"luca","DEVICE1","30494","242196","wipe device",
"damien","DEVICE2","119382","242533","wipe device",
"angel","DEVICE3","187654","242533","delete device",
"mattias","DESKTOP6-RRT","50352","242165","wipe script",
"nicklas","TEST1","21038","242181","delete device",
"stephen","TEST2","29123","242921","delete script",
"franck","MYCOMP","196123","242533","wipe device",
"christophe","HELLOWORLD","7859","242551","delete device"
];
```

3. In a new column, DiskState, add text as below:
   - If FreePercent < 20% then DiskState="Low disk space"
   - Else DiskState="Disk space OK"
4. Filter records where DiskState = "Low disk space"
5. Filter on records where actions are wipe or delete or remediation scripts and add value in a new column

Intune environment

1. Use the IntuneDevices log and the previous query to get free disk percent
2. Do the same than in "demo lab env" part 3, 4, 5

🔍 Key words

- iff,iif, extend

 # DAY 12

Exercises of the day

Demo lab environment

1. Open aka.ms/LADemo
2. In a new query create a variable A with value 5
3. Display the content of the variable A
4. Now, create a variable A with value 10, and B with value 5
5. Multiply both variable A and B and display the result
6. Use the datatable from the day 8 part 1
7. Using the query to get FreePercent, create variable RequiredFreeSpace with value 30 and display devices where FreePercent is lesser than the RequiredFreeSpace

Intune environment

1. In IntuneDevices, create a variable RequiredFreeSpace with value 30
2. Using the query to get FreePercent, display devices where percent is lesser than the variable RequiredFreeSpace

Key words

- let, print
- ago

 DAY 13

🗞 Exercises of the day

Demo lab environment

1. Open aka.ms/LADemo
2. Use the below datatable
3. Display records where LastContact column is < than 7 days
4. Why is there an error?
5. Convert the LastContact column to a date
6. Format the date as: MM/dd/yyyy
7. Create a variable Date = '2023-12-18'
8. In a new variable DateFormat, convert variable to a date
9. In a new variable, Today, add the date of today
10. Format the date as: month/day/year
11. Add 6 hours to the variable Today
12. Format the variable Today to different time zone

Intune environment

1. Use the IntuneDevices log
2. Do the same than in "demo lab env" part 3, 4, 5, 6, 7, 8, 9, 10, 11, 12

🔍 Key words

- datetime, make_datetime, format_datetime, datetime_add
- let, now(), datetime_local_to_utc

DAY 14

Exercises of the day

1. Open aka.ms/LADemo
2. Create a variable Today, containing the date of today
3. Create a variable CustomDate with the following date value 2023-12-19 (in a date format of course)
4. Create a variable DateDiff and calculate the difference between Today and CustomDate
5. Convert the previous result to a number of days

Key words

- datetime, datetime_diff
- extend, now()

 # DAY 15

🖥️ Exercises of the day

Demo lab environment

1. Open aka.ms/LADemo
2. Use the below datatable

```
let Devices=datatable
(username:string,device:string,LastContact:string,StorageFree:long,
StorageTotal:long)
[
"luca","DEVICE1","2024-06-29 22:03:42.0000000","7859","242551",
"damien","DEVICE2","2024-09-29 21:36:42.0000000","7859","242551",
"angel","DEVICE3","2024-10-04 22:02:42.0000000","196123","242533",
"mattias","DESKTOP6-RRT","2023-05-01
22:00:42.0000000","149965","241921",
"nicklas","TEST1","2024-10-01 21:53:42.0000000","187654","242533"
];
```

3. Display records where last contact is between 5 and 9 days (different methods)
4. Display records where last contact is between today and 7 days
5. Calculate free disk percent and display devices where percent is between 0% and 5%

Intune environment

1. In the IntuneDevices table
2. Do the same than in "demo lab env" part 3, 4, 5

🔍 Key words

- ago, between
- make_datetime

 # DAY 16

👨‍🏫 Exercises of the day

1. Open aka.ms/LADemo
2. Use the below query to create a specific table of data
```
datatable (Action:string)
[
"Executed by Damien Van Robaeys",
"Executed by Luca Van Robaeys"
]
```
3. Extract only the username, data after string "Executed by"
4. Extract only the username, data after string "by"
5. Use the below query to create a specific table of data
```
datatable (Action:string)
[
"Program=Powershell;User=Damien Van Robaeys (DESKTOP-TST)",
"Program=python;User=Luca Van Robaeys (DESKTOP-TST2)",
]
```
6. Extract value after "Program" in a new a column "Program"
7. Extract both values "Program" and "User" in new columns
8. Create a variable to get the computer name between the "()"
9. In the SigninLogs log, use the "in" operator to filter on the following ResultType: 50126, 50133, 50144, 50133
10. Using parse operator, get following information from the AuthenticationDetails column: authenticationStepDateTime authenticationMethod

🔍 Key words

- parse
- in

 DAY 17

🎦 Exercises of the day

1. Open aka.ms/LADemo
2. Use the below query to create a specific datatable
datatable (Devices:string)
[
'{"username": "damien van robaeys","device":
"DESKTOP_TEST","manufacturer": "lenovo","model":"T480s"}',
'{"username": "luca van robaeys","Device":
"DESKTOP_TST2","manufacturer": "lenovo","model":"T14s
Gen4"}'
]
3. Extract username, devicename, manufacturer and model in different columns
4. In the SecurityEvent log parse the EventData column
5. Extract following info in different columns: PolicyName and FilePath
6. Filter records where UserData is not empty

🔍 Key words

- parse_json, parse_xml, todynamic
- datatable, isnotempty

 DAY 18

👨‍🏫 Exercises of the day

1. Open aka.ms/LADemo
2. Use the below datatable

```
Let
Devices=datatable(username:string,device:string,version:string)
[
        "luca","DEVICE1","17.1.4",
        "damien","DEVICE2","16.4.3",
        "angel","DEVICE3","16.5.1",
        "mattias","DESKTOP6-RRT","15.3.7 ",
        "nicklas","TEST1","15.2.1"
];
```

3. Filter on devices where version is 17.1.2 or something else
4. Filter now on version 17.1.2 or 16.5.1 or something else
5. Display devices where version is lesser than 15.3.7 or something else

🔍 Key words

- contains, in, extend
- parse_version

 DAY 19

Exercises of the day

1. Open aka.ms/LADemo
2. In a new query, create a variable var1 with value "hello"
3. Add a variable var2 with value "world"
4. Concatenate both variables
5. In a new query, create a variable longvalue with value 20L80004
6. In a new variable shortvalue, split the variable longvalue to keep the last 4 characters
7. In a new query add a variable user with the following email damien.vanrobaeys@gmail.com
8. In a new variable user_split, split the user variable to keep values before the @ character
9. In a new variable username, get the part before the @ from the user_split variable
10. Create a variable with the following path
"C:\Users\damien.vanrobaeys\AppData\Local\Microsoft\Outlook"
11. Display content of the variable
12. Why is there an error?
13. Escape the \ character to display the variable
14. Split the variable to show only the user name

Q Key words

- split, let
- strcat, substring, //

DAY 20

Exercises of the day

Demo lab environment

1. Open aka.ms/LADemo
2. Use the below datatable

```
let Devices=datatable
(username:string,device:string,StorageFree:long,StorageTotal
:long)
[
"luca","DEVICE1","30494","242196",
"damien","DEVICE2","119382","242533",
"angel","DEVICE3","187654","242533",
"mattias","DESKTOP6-RRT","50352","242165",
"nicklas","TEST1","21038","242181",
"stephen","TEST2","29123","242921",
"franck","MYCOMP","196123","242533"];
```

3. Depending on the percent create a new column DiskState and add text as below using the case function:
   - Above 5%: FreePercent < 5%
   - Between 5%-20%: FreePercent between 5% and 20%
   - Between 20%-50%: FreePercent between 20% and 50%
   - Above 50%: FreePercent greater than 50%

Intune environment

1. Use the IntuneDevices log and the query to get the free disk percent
2. Do the same than in "demo lab env" part 3

Q Key words

- case, let, extend

 DAY 21

🖼️ Exercises of the day

1. Open aka.ms/LADemo
2. Use the below datatable

```
let Devices=datatable
(username:string,device:string,StorageFree:long,StorageTotal
:long)
[
        "luca","DEVICE1","20NYSCP900",
        "damien","DEVICE2","20T1S20700",
        "angel","DEVICE3","20T1S20700",
        "mattias","DESKTOP6-RRT","20NYSCP900",
        "nicklas","TEST1","21BSS20L00",
        "stephen","TEST2","20L8S2AV00",
        "franck","MYCOMP","20WNS2UG00",
        "christophe","HELLOWORLD","20WNS2UG00"
];
```

3. In a new column MTM, split the Model column to keep only the first 4 characters
4. Add a new column FriendlyName and replace MTM with something more understandable as below:
   - 20L8 with ThinkPad T480s
   - 20T1 with ThinkPad T14s
   - 20WN with ThinkPad T14s Gen2
   - 21BS with ThinkPad T14s Gen3
   - 20NY with ThinkPad T490s

🔍 Key words

- replace, replace_strings
- dynamic

 DAY 22

Exercises of the day

1. Open aka.ms/LADemo
2. Use the following datatable

```
let Devices=datatable (username: string, device: string,
Model: string)
    [
    "luca", "DEVICE1", "20NYSCP900",
    "damien", "DEVICE2", "20T1S20700",
    "angel", "DEVICE3", "20T1S20700",
    "mattias", "DESKTOP6-RRT", "20NYSCP900",
    "nicklas", "TEST1", "21BSS20L00",
    "luca", "TEST2", "20L8S2AV00",
    "damien", "MYCOMP", "20WNS2UG00",
    "christophe", "HELLOWORLD", "20T1S20700"
];
```

3. Count numbers of devices where model equals 20L8
4. Count number of devices by model
5. Display the result in a Pie chart
6. Sort order on devices count
7. Count the number of devices per user
8. Filter on user with more than 1 device

Q Key words

- summarize, by, count
- render, piechart

 DAY 23

Exercises of the day

1. Open aka.ms/LADemo
2. Create a new variable Devices
3. In this variable, create a data table of values as below:
❖ Columns: devicename, username, manufacturer
❖ All columns are strings
▪ Row1: Computer1, damien.vanrobaeys, lenovo
▪ Row2: Computer2, luca.vanrobaeys, lenovo
▪ Row3: Computer3, walter.white, lenovo
▪ Row4: Computer1, jessie.pinkman, lenovo

4. In a variable, BSOD, create a table of values as below:
❖ Columns: devicename, BSODCount, BSODCode, Model, BIOSVersion
❖ All columns are strings except BSODCount (integer)
▪ Row1: Computer1,4,0x000000A0, ThinkPad T480s,1.49
▪ Row2: Computer2,1,0x00000116, ThinkPad T14s,1.24
▪ Row3: Computer3,15,0x000000A0, ThinkPad T14s Gen2,1.50
▪ Row4: Computer4,0,0x00000154, ThinkPad T14s Gen3,1.50
▪ Row5: Computer5,2,0x00000154, ThinkPad T14s,1.24
▪ Row6: Computer6,5,0x00000154, ThinkPad T480s,1.49
▪ Row7: Computer7,10,0x00000154, ThinkPad T490s,1.49

5. Display content of the BSOD variable
6. In the BSOD log, filter on records with model ThinkPad T480s
7. In the BSOD log, filter on records with more than 5 BSOD

Key words

▪ Let, datatable

 DAY 24

👨‍🏫 Exercises of the day

1. Open aka.ms/LADemo
2. Use both previous Devices and BSOD variables
3. What is common value between both tables?
4. What is the column that you can use to join both tables?
5. Join both devices and BSOD tables
6. What did you notice about the common field?
7. Remove the common column from the BSOD table
8. Now use the following datatables

```
let BSOD=datatable
(device:string,BSODCount:int,BSODCode:string,Model:string)
[
"Computer1","4","0x000000A0","ThinkPad T480s","1.49",
"Computer2","1","0x00000116","ThinkPad T14s","1.24 ",
];
let Devices=datatable
(computer:string,user:string,manufacturer:string)
[
"Computer1","damien.vanrobaeys","lenovo",
"Computer2","luca.vanrobaeys","lenovo",
"Computer3","walter.white","dell",
"Computer4","jessie.pinkman","lenovo",
"Computer5","gustavo.fringe","hp",
];
```

9. What did you notice between both tables?
10. Join both tables (two ways)

🔍 Key words

- Join, left, right
- away, project-away

 DAY 25

🧑‍🏫 Exercises of the day

1. Open aka.ms/LADemo
2. Use the previous query with devices and BSOD tables
3. What did you notice in the fields from the devices table, after joining both tables?
4. Change the join type using the kind attribute with inner and innerunique value
5. What did you notice?
6. Test other kind

🔍 Key words

- let, inner, innerunique, fullouter, leftouter
- join, kind

DAY 26

Exercises of the day

1. Open aka.ms/LADemo
2. Use the previous query with Devices and BSOD tables
3. Join both tables only for devices with more than 5 BSOD

Key words

- let
- join, where

 DAY 27

📽 Exercises of the day

1. Open aka.ms/LADemo
2. Join both devices and BSOD tables using the union operator instead of the join operator
3. What did you notice?
4. Join both devices and BSOD tables using the lookup operator instead of the join operator
5. What did you notice?

🔍 Key words

- union, lookup

 DAY 28

Exercises of the day

1. Open aka.ms/LADemo
2. In the following exercise you have different workspace, test1 and test2
3. From the workspace test1, join table Devices from the workspace test2
4. Join table Devices from test2 on the DeviceName property
5. Display records for Lenovo devices from the last 7 days from the test1 workspace

Key words

- workspace, join
- summarize, isnotempty

 DAY 29

👨‍🏫 Exercises of the day

1. Open aka.ms/LADemo
2. Download the BIOS_lab.json file from here
   https://github.com/damienvanrobaeys/Learn-KQL-in-one-
   month/blob/main/ExternalData/BIOS_lab.json
3. Upload the file somewhere like Azure blob storage
4. Load the data from the uploaded JSON with KQL
5. Use the below JSON link from my GitHub
   https://raw.githubusercontent.com/damienvanrobaeys/Learn-
   KQL-in-one-month/master/ExternalData/BIOS_lab.json
6. Load data directly from the JSON on my GitHub

🔍 Key words

- externaldata, with, h
- datatable

 # DAY 30

🖥️ Exercises of the day

1. Open aka.ms/LADemo
2. Use the below JSON link from my GitHub
   https://raw.githubusercontent.com/damienvanrobaeys/Learn-KQL-in-one-month/master/ExternalData/Devices.json
3. Load the data from the JSON with KQL
4. Join the previous Devices table to the external data
5. Use the below JSON link from my GitHub
   https://raw.githubusercontent.com/damienvanrobaeys/Learn-KQL-in-one-month/master/ExternalData/BSOD.json
6. Load the data from the JSON with KQL
7. Join both data from both JSON files

🔍 Key words

- externaldata, with, h
- datatable

 DAY 31

🖼️ Exercises of the day

1. Open aka.ms/LADemo
2. Decode the following base64 code to a string:
'SGVsbG8sIHdlbGNvbWUgaW4gdGhlICJMZWFybiBLUUwgaW4gb2
5IIG1vbnRoIiBib29rLCAyMDI1IGVkaXRpb24uCkhvcGUgeW91Ugd
2lsbCBlbmpveSBpdA=='
3. Encode the below string to base64:
    Hello, let's encode me to base64
4. Geolocate the following IP address: 20.53.203.50
5. Extract values country, state and city
6. In the WindowsFirewall log, filter on private IP address
7. In the SecurityEvent log, filter on eventid 4688 (a new
    process has been created), where commandline is powershell
    and contains encodedcommand
8. Parse commandline to extract the encoded command in a new
    variable
9. Decode the encoded command in the new variable from
    base64 to a string

🔍 Key words

- ipv4_is_private
- geo_info_from_ip_address
- datatable, parse, let
- base64_decode_tostring, base64_encode_tostring

Solution

Intune environment

1. Display all data from IntuneDevices log

To display all records from a log, here IntuneDevices, there are two ways:
- Go to **LogManagement** > double-click on **IntuneDevices**
- Go the query editor, type **IntuneDevices** > click on **Run**

This will show all data (rows and columns) from the IntuneDevices table/log:

2. Display all columns but just change order by displaying LastContact in the first place

As you may notice on the previous picture, by default the **TimeGenerated** column is displayed at the first place.

If you want to change the order, we need to use the **project** operator.
This one allows you to choose which column to display. Here we just want to change the order, so we will add **reorder** to the **project** operator, as below:

```
Table
| project-reorder Column1Name, Column2Name,…
```

You can also specify the column name to put at the first place and let all other columns after, as below:

Table
```
| project-reorder LastContact, *
```

You may notice that when you start typing **| project**, this automatically displays options available for this operator, as below:

Then we just need to specify the order, here column **LastContact** at the first place, so it will be as below:

IntuneDevices
```
| project-reorder LastContact
```
Or
IntuneDevices
```
| project-reorder LastContact, *
```

The result will be the following:

3. Hide the following columns: OperationName, Result, GraphDeviceIsManaged

Instead of changing the order we need to remove some columns from the default displaying.

For that, add **away** to the **project** operator, as below:

```
IntuneDevices
| project-away OperationName,Result,GraphDeviceIsManaged
```

7. Show schema of the log meaning columns type

You can easily display type of each column in a log, meaning see the schema of the log or table.
For that just explore the log through the portal by extending it.
Here is the example with the IntuneDevices log:

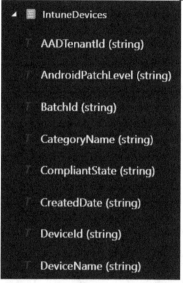

It shows the name of the column and the type of the column like DeviceName which is a string.

You can also do this through a KQL query using the **getschema** operator.
This one can be used as below:

```
Table
| getschema
```

Here is the query for the **IntuneDevices** log:

```
IntuneDevices
| getschema
```

See below the result:

ColumnName	ColumnOrdinal	DataType	···	ColumnType
> TenantId	0	System.String		string
> TimeGenerated	1	System.DateTime		datetime
> OperationName	2	System.String		string
> Result	3	System.String		string
> SourceSystem	4	System.String		string
> DeviceId	5	System.String		string

Results   Chart (above)

This will show same result than through the portal.

8. Get type of the LastContact column with KQL then portal

You can then easily get the type for a specific column by filtering on the ColumnName column as below:

```
IntuneDevices
| getschema
| where ColumnName == "LastContact"
```

See below the result:

Results   Chart

ColumnName	ColumnOrdinal	DataType	ColumnType
> LastContact	8	System.String	string

9. Get type of following values: a, 111, 1=1, now(), 1s

Here we have different values, and we want to see type of those values. For that we can use gettype(), as below:

```
gettype("Value to check")
```

See below gettype queries for our need:
```
print gettype("a")
print gettype(111)
print gettype(1=1)
print gettype(now())
```

See below result for each query:

Query	Result
gettype("a")	string
gettype(111)	Long
gettype(1=1)	Bool
gettype(now())	datetime

Demo lab environment

2. Display all data from the SecurityEvent log

To display all content of a log, here SecurityEvent, there are two ways:
- Go to **Microsoft Sentinel** > double-click on **SecurityEvent**
- Go the query editor, type **SecurityEvent** > click on **Run**

This will show all data meaning all columns from table/log:

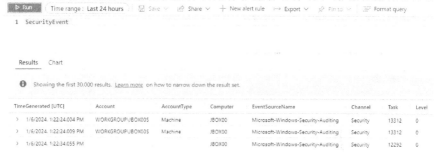

3. Display all columns but just change order by displaying Activity in the first place

As you may notice on the previous picture, by default the **TimeGenerated** column is displayed at the first place.

If you want to change the order, we need to use the project operator.
This one allows you to choose which column to display.
Here we just want to change the order, so we will add **reorder** to the **project** operator, as below:

```
Table
| project-reorder Column1Name, Column2Name,…
```

You can also specify the column name to put at the first place and let all other columns after, as below:

`Table | project-reorder LastContact, *`

You may notice that when you start typing | project, this automatically display options available for this operator, as below:

Then we just need to specify the order, here column **Activity** at the first place, so it will be as below:

SecurityEvent
| project-reorder Activity
Or
SecurityEvent
| project-reorder Activity, *

The result will be the following:

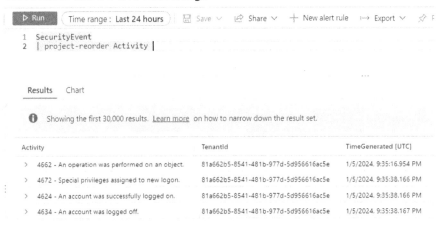

4. Hide the following columns: EventSourceName, Channel, AdditionalInfo, AdditionalInfo2, AuthenticationPackageName

Instead of changing the order we want to remove some columns from the default displaying.
For that we will add **away** to the **project** operator, as below:

```
SecurityEvent
| project-away EventSourceName,Channel,
AdditionalInfo,AdditionalInfo2,AuthenticationPackageName
```

10. Show schema of the log meaning columns type

You can easily display type of each column in a log, meaning see the schema of the log or table.
For that just explore the log through the portal by extending it.
Here is the example with the SecurityEvent log:

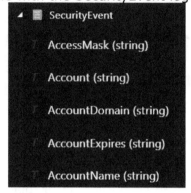

It shows the name of the column and the type of the column like Account which is a string.
You can also do this through a KQL query using the **getschema** operator.
This one can be used as below:

```
Table | getschema
```

Here is the query for the **SecurityEvent** log:

```
SecurityEvent | getschema
```

See below the result:

ColumnName	ColumnOrdinal	DataType	ColumnType
> TenantId	0	System.String	string
> TimeGenerated	1	System.DateTime	datetime
> SourceSystem	2	System.String	string
> Account	3	System.String	string
> AccountType	4	System.String	string

This will show same result than through the portal.

11. Get type of the Channel column with KQL then portal

You can then easily get the type for a specific column by filtering on the Channel column as below:

```
SecurityEvent
| getschema
| where ColumnName == "Channel"
```

See below the result:

ColumnName	ColumnOrdi...	DataType	ColumnType
> Channel	7	System.String	string

12. Get type of following values: a, 111, 1=1, now(), 1s

Here we have different values, and we want to see type of those values. For that we can use gettype(), as below:

```
gettype("Value to check")
```

See below gettype queries for our need:
```
print gettype("a")
print gettype(111)
print gettype(1=1)
print gettype(now())
```

See below result for each query:

Query	Result
gettype("a")	string
gettype(111)	Long
gettype(1=1)	Bool
gettype(now())	datetime

 DAY 2

Intune environment

1. In the IntuneDevices log, display only the following columns: TimeGenerated, LastContact, DeviceName, Model, SerialNumber,UserName,upn

As mentioned on first day to choose what to display we need to use the **project** operator.
To display only some specific columns, just type **project** then columns to display as below for our exercise:

```
IntuneDevices
| project TimeGenerated, LastContact, DeviceName, Model,
SerialNumber,UserName,UPN
```

2. Display results from the last hour

From the query editor
As you may notice, by default result will display records from the last 24 hours, look here Time range:

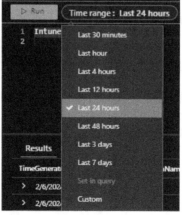

You can change it by clicking on the **Time range** button:

Now let's select Last hour and click the on the **Run** button.
This will show records from the last hour.

Directly in your query
Instead of selecting the time range from the button, we will modify it directly in the query.
To proceed we need to use the **ago()** function on the **TimeGenerated** property.

We need now to check all records that occurred during the last 1 hour, meaning where **TimeGenerated** is greater than 1 hour. The KQL query to use will be the following:

```
IntuneDevices
| where TimeGenerated > ago(1h)
```

3. Display results from the last 7 days

From the query editor
Just click on the Time range button and select Last 7 days then click the on Run button.
This will now show records from the last 7 days.

Directly in your query
Just like before we will use the ago() function and just replace 1h with 7d where d means day.

```
IntuneDevices
| where TimeGenerated > ago(7d)
```

Demo lab environment

2. In the SecurityEvent log, display only the following columns: TimeGenerated,Account,Computer,EventID,Activity

As mentioned on first day to choose what to display we need to use the **project** operator.
To display only some specific columns, just type **project** then columns to display as below for our exercise:

```
SecurityEvent
| project TimeGenerated,Account,Computer,EventID,Activity
```

3. Display results from the last hour

From the query editor

As you may notice, by default result displays records from the last 24 hours, look here Time range:

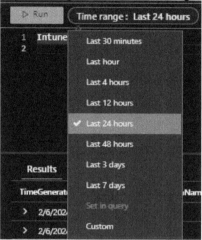

You can change it by clicking on the Time range button:

Now let's select Last hour and click the on Run button.
This will show records from the last hour.

Directly in your query

Now instead of selecting the time range from the button, we will modify it directly in the query.
To proceed we need to use the **ago()** function on the **TimeGenerated** column.

We need now to check all records that occurred during the last 1 hour, meaning where **TimeGenerated** is greater than 1 hour. The KQL query to use will be the following:

```
SecurityEvent
| where TimeGenerated > ago(1h)
```

4. Display results from the last 7 days

From the query editor

Just click on the **Time range** button, select **Last 7 days** then click on **Run**.

This will now show records from the last 7 days.

Directly in your query
Just like before we will use the **ago()** function and just replace
1h with **7d** where d means day.

```
SecurityEvent
| where TimeGenerated > ago(7d)
```

 DAY 3

Demo lab environment

2. Use the below datatable
```
let Devices=datatable
(username:string,devicename:string,serialnumber:string)
[
"luca","DEVICE1","E3QTSY",
"damien","DEVICE2","AZJTOL"
];
```
3. Rename columns as below:
   - username: user
   - devicename: device
   - SerialNumber: SN

By default, when you display content of a table, columns are displayed with their default name.
Sometimes default name may be a bit not understandable in a dashboard.
To rename a column, there are two ways:
- Add **rename** to the **project** operator
- Just type new name **==** old name

Here below we will rename some columns using **project-rename**:

```
Devices
| project-rename
User=username,device=devicename,SN=serialnumber
```

You can also use project operator as below:

```
| project User=username,device=devicename,SN=serialnumber
```

See below the result:

79

4. Rename columns by adding blank space as below:
   - username: user name
   - devicename: device name
   - serialumber: serial number
   - model: model

In the first part, we have renamed column but now let's add blank space.

For that just add the new column name in bracket as following: ['new name']=oldname

See below the query from the first part but with space:

```
Devices
| project-rename ['User name']=username,['Device
name']=devicename,['Serial number']=serialnumber
```

See below the result:

User name	Device name	Serial number
> luca	DEVICE1	E3QTSY
> damien	DEVICE2	AZJTOL

 # DAY 4

Intune environment

1. Use the previous query, and filter on the device name by clicking on the DeviceName column header
2. There are many records for the same device, why?

That's because all devices have many records for all activity with Log Analytics meaning you will see different records with different **TimeGenerated** values for a same device.

3. On the last 7 days, keep only the latest result for each device

We want, here, to keep only the last result for all devices.
For that we will use the **summarize** operator using the **arg_max** function.
You can get more information about this function on the below link:
https://learn.microsoft.com/en-us/azure/data-explorer/kusto/query/arg-max-aggfunction

The **arg_max** function allows you to get the maximum value from a column. If you use it with a time value, it will help you to get the last time a record had an activity.
The KQL query will be the following:

```
| summarize arg_max(TimeGenerated)
```

We will then specify to filter on the DeviceName column to get the last time that a device had an activity.
The KQL query will be the following:

```
IntuneDevices
| summarize arg_max(TimeGenerated,*) by DeviceName
```

4. Display only 10 records randomly

Here we want to limit results to only 10 records and we want to get them randomly.

For that two operators can be used: limit or take.
To use them just specify the operator and the count of records, as below:

```
| limit or take count (like 10)
```

See below the KQL query with **limit**:

```
IntuneDevices
| summarize arg_max(TimeGenerated,*) by DeviceName
| limit 10
```

See below the KQL query with **take**:

```
IntuneDevices
| summarize arg_max(TimeGenerated,*) by DeviceName
| take 10
```

Demo lab environment

2. Use the previous query, and filter on the device name by clicking on the Account column header
3. There are many records for the same device, why?

That's because each device will have many records for all activity with Log Analytics meaning you will see different records with different **TimeGenerated** values for a same device.

4. On the last 7 days, keep only the latest result for each account

Here we want to keep only the last result for all devices.
For that we will use the **summarize** operator using the **arg_max** function.
You can get more information about this function on the below link:
https://learn.microsoft.com/en-us/azure/data-explorer/kusto/query/arg-max-aggfunction

The **arg_max** function allows you to get the maximum value from a column. If you use it with a time value, it will help you to get the last time a record had an activity.

The KQL query will be the following:

```
| summarize arg_max(TimeGenerated)
```

We will then specify to filter on the Account column to get the last time that a device had an activity.
The KQL query will be the following:

```
SecurityEvent
| summarize arg_max(TimeGenerated,*) by Account
```

5. Display only 10 records randomly

We want, here, to limit results to only 10 records and we want to get them randomly.
For that two operators can be used: **limit** or **take**.
To use them just specify the operator and the count of records, as below:

```
| limit or take count (like 10)
```

See below the KQL query with **limit**:

```
SecurityEvent
| summarize arg_max(TimeGenerated,*) by Account
| limit 10
```

See below the KQL query with **take**:

```
SecurityEvent
| summarize arg_max(TimeGenerated,*) by Account
| take 10
```

 DAY 5

2. Use the below datatable
3. Search everything containing word "luca"

Using **where** operator, you can search if a specific property contains a specific value or a list of values.

Here we want to look for a specific word, string in the table. This word can exist in any columns not only in a specific one.

For that we will use the **search** operator. That can be used as below:

```
search in (table) "value to search"
```

Notre that it's the same than using query as following:

```
Table
| search "value to search"
```

Here we want to search every row containing the string "luca". For that the search operator can be used as below:

```
search in (Devices) "luca"
```

See below the result:

$table	username	device	manufacturer	model
> search_arg0	luca	DEVICE1	LENOVO	T14s Gen1

4. Do the same with word "LENOVO" or "lenovo"

Now we want to search every row containing the word "LENOVO" in the table Devices.
We will use the same query than before as below:

```
search in (Devices) "lenovo"
```

See below the result:

username	device	manufacturer ⋯	model
luca	DEVICE1	LENOVO	T14s Gen1
damien	DEVICE2	lenovo	T14s
stephen	TEST2	Lenovo	T14s Gen 3
stephen	TEST2	Lenovo	T14s Gen 3
christophe	TEST3	lenovo	T14s gen4
evrard	TEST3	lenovo	T14s Gen2
myriam	DKTP-123	lenovo	T14S Gen2

Here below is the result with word "LENOVO":

username	device	manufacturer ⋯	model
luca	DEVICE1	LENOVO	T14s Gen1
damien	DEVICE2	lenovo	T14s
stephen	TEST2	Lenovo	T14s Gen 3
stephen	TEST2	Lenovo	T14s Gen 3
christophe	TEST3	lenovo	T14s gen4
evrard	TEST3	lenovo	T14s Gen2
myriam	DKTP-123	lenovo	T14S Gen2

5. What did you notice?

By default, the search operator is case insensitive, meaning whatever you type with uppercase or lowercase it will return the same result. Researching "lenovo", "LENOVO" or "Lenovo" will return the same thing.

6. Make the research case-sensitive

If you want to search for a specific word with an exact value, we will add some case-sensitive to our query. For that we will just add a kind as below:

```
search kind=case_sensitive in (Devices) "lenovo"
```

See below the result:

username	device	manufacturer	model
damien	DEVICE2	lenovo	T14s
christophe	TEST3	lenovo	T14s gen4
evrard	TEST3	lenovo	T14s Gen2
myriam	DKTP-123	lenovo	T14S Gen2

7. Add the below datatable
8. Search for luca in both tables

The search operator also allows you to look for value in multiple tables, as below:

```
search in (table1,table2,…) "value to search"
```

In this example we want to search the word "luca" in the following tables: Devices and Devices2.

```
search in (Devices,Devices2) "luca"
```

See below the result:

	$table	username	device	manufacturer	model
>	search_arg0	luca	DEVICE1	LENOVO	T14s Gen1
>	search_arg1	luca	DEVICE1	LENOVO	T14s Gen1

Results   Chart

9. In the Devices table remove duplicated rows

To get a list of unique values in a column, the operator to use is distinct. It allows you to remove duplicated entries for a specific column.
It works as below:

```
Table | distinct ColumnName,ColumnName2, ...
```

In the Devices table we have two rows with the same values:
"stephen","TEST2","Lenovo","T14s Gen 3",
"stephen","TEST2","Lenovo","T14s Gen 3",

Now to get only one row instead of two, the distinct operator can be used as below:

```
Devices
| distinct device, username
```

 DAY 6

2. Use the below query to create a Devices datatable
3. Display records with word lenovo using has

The **has** operator can be used to search if a string contains a specific pattern, a specific term or word (three or more characters). To proceed, we will first use **where** operator and filter on a property with a specific value, as below:

`Table | where Column has (Pattern)`

Here we want to look for the word "lenovo" in the whole table, meaning the has query will be the following:

`Devices | where data has ("lenovo")`

See below the result:

data
> {"username": "damien","device": "LENO_TST1","manufacturer": "lenovo","model":"T480s","SN":"TR6EYN"}
> {"username": "luca","device": "LENO_TST3","manufacturer": "LENOVO","model":"T14s","SN":"TERY67"}

It returns three rows, which is exactly the number of rows with the word Lenovo.

4. Display records with word LENOVO using has

Here we will do the same than before using "LENOVO" in uppercase:

`Devices | where data has ("LENOVO")`

See below the result:

data
> {"username": "damien","device": "LENO_TST1","manufacturer": "lenovo","model":"T480s","SN":"TR6EYN"}
> {"username": "luca","device": "LENO_TST3","manufacturer": "LENOVO","model":"T14s","SN":"TERY67"}

5. What did you notice?

The result is the same if we type "lenovo" or "LENOVO" meaning the has operator is case insensitive and we can look for a string with uppercase or lowercase.
You can see in the result from part 2. That it returns rows containing word "lenovo" as well as "LENOVO".

6. Display records with word lenovo or dell using has_any

We want to look for results where the string contains "lenovo" OR "dell".
As we have seen before the **has** operator helps us to look for a specific word.
Now to search for one word or more we will use the **has_any** operator.
This operator works as below:

```
Table | where Column has_any ("Pattern1","Pattern2",…)
```

The KQL query to search results with word "Lenovo" or "dell" is:

```
Devices | where data has_any ("lenovo","dell")
```

See below the result:

```
>   {"username": "damien","device": "LENO_TST1","manufacturer": "lenovo","model":"T480s","SN":"TR6EYN"}
>   {"username": "luca","device": "LENO_TST3","manufacturer": "LENOVO","model":"T14s","SN":"TERY67"}
>   {"username": "angel","device": "TEST","manufacturer": "dell","model":"XPS 15","SN":"U8INYN"}
>   {"username": "mattias","device": "DELL1","manufacturer": "Dell","model":"XPS 13","SN":""}
```

We have here five rows, for Lenovo or dell.
As you may noticed, it will return result if it contains lenovo, LENOVO, Dell or dell meaning it's still case insensitive.

7. Display records with word lenovo and luca using has_all

Now instead of searching for a word a or word b we want to get results where a string contains exactly multiple words, here "lenovo" and "luca".
For that, the operator to use is **has_all** and works as below:

```
Table | where Column has_all ("Pattern1","Pattern2",…)
```

It will then return the line containing both words Pattern1 and Pattern2.

Our KQL query is now:

```
Devices | where data has_all ("lenovo","luca")
```

The result is one row as below:

data
> {"username": "luca","device": "LENO_TST3","manufacturer": "LENOVO","model":"T14s","SN":"TERY67"}

8. Display records with word lenovo using contains

In the number 2, we filtered records with value "lenovo" using the **has** operator. Now let's do the same using the **contains** operator. This operator works as below:

```
Table | where ColumnName contains "Pattern"
```

Pattern is the name of the string that should be in the main string, here "lenovo".
Our KQL will be the following:

```
Devices | where data contains "lenovo"
```

See below the result:

> {"username": "damien","device": "LENO_TST1","manufacturer": "lenovo","model":"T480s","SN":"TR6EYN"}
> {"username": "luca","device": "LENO_TST3","manufacturer": "LENOVO","model":"T14s","SN":"TERY67"}

It returns three rows, which is exactly the number of rows with the word Lenovo.

9. Display records with word LENOVO using contains

Here we will do the same than before using "LENOVO" in uppercase:

```
Devices | where data contains ("LENOVO")
```

See below the result:

> {"username": "damien","device": "LENO_TST1","manufacturer": "lenovo","model":"T480s","SN":"TR6EYN"}
> {"username": "luca","device": "LENO_TST3","manufacturer": "LENOVO","model":"T14s","SN":"TERY67"}

10. What did you notice?

The result is the same if we type "lenovo" or "LENOVO" meaning the contains operator is case insensitive and we can look for a string with uppercase or lowercase.

11. Display records with word lenovo or dell using contains

To search for multiple strings using contains operator we need to add multiple contains filter (one by string to search).
Our contains filtering will be as following:

```
Devices
| where data contains "lenovo" or data contains "dell"
```

Result is the below one:

> {"username": "damien","device": "LENO_TST1","manufacturer": "lenovo","model":"T480s","SN":"TR6EYN"}

> {"username": "luca","device": "LENO_TST3","manufacturer": "LENOVO","model":"T14s","SN":"TERY67"}

> {"username": "angel","device": "TEST","manufacturer": "dell","model":"XPS 15","SN":"U8INYN"}

> {"username": "mattias","device": "DELL1","manufacturer": "Dell","model":"XPS 13","SN":""}

12. Display records with word "lenovo" and "luca" using contains

Now we want to get result where data contains exactly some specific strings using a AND, as below:

```
Devices
| where data contains "lenovo" and data contains "luca"
```

The result is only one row:

data

> {"username": "luca","device": "LENO_TST3","manufacturer": "LENOVO","model":"T14s","SN":"TERY67"}

13. What did you notice between has and contains?

Filtering on multiple strings using contains operator can become a bit complex if you have many things to add to your search. Here we look for two words, "lenovo" or "dell". We have two contains operator in our query.

```
Devices
| where data contains "lenovo" or data contains "dell"
```
If we want to add some other filters, we need to add other contains.

For instance, let's filter result containing one of the following words: lenovo, dell, T14s, XPS 13.
Our query will be:

```
Devices
| where data contains "lenovo" or data contains "dell" or
data contains "T14s" or data contains "XPS 13"
```

As you can see, we have where data contains a or data contains b or data contains c or data contains d...
The query can become very long.

Using the has operator now, the previous query would be as below:

```
Devices
| where data has_any("lenovo","dell","T14s","XPS 13")
```

As you may noticed it is less complex to understand and manage.

14. Display records with word lenovo using "=="

The equals operator (==) works like the contains:

```
Table | where ColumnName == "Pattern"
```

Now we want to use the equals operator to get result by filtering on the "lenovo" word.
See below the query:

```
Devices | where data == "lenovo"
```

15. What did you notice?

Using the above query, result is empty.
That's because the equals operator (==) is used to search for an exact string.
Here the string contains the word lenovo but not exactly lenovo meaning not only lenovo.

16. Use the below query to create a new table with fake data
17. Display records where manufacturer is Lenovo with "=="

We have seen how to use the equals operator. Now we have different columns and want to filter result where a column (Manufacturer) contains a specific value (lenovo).
The KQL query is the following:

```
Devices | where manufacturer == "lenovo"
```

The result shows two rows:

username	device	manufacturer	model	SN
> kevin	LENO_TST3	lenovo	T14s	TERY67

Weird you may thing given that we have three rows where manufacturer is "lenovo".

18. Do the same with manufacturer "Lenovo"

See below the query:

```
Devices | where manufacturer == "Lenovo"
```

See below the result:

username	device	manufacturer	model	SN
> luca	LENO_TST2	Lenovo	T14s	

19. What did you notice?

By default, the equals operator is case sensitive that's why filtering on "lenovo" returns only two rows instead of three.

20. Display records where Manufacturer is "lenovo" or "LENOVO" using contains

As we have seen before, by default the contains operator is case insensitive, meaning filtering on lenovo, Lenovo, LENOVO is the same and will return the same result.

See below the query:

```
Devices | where manufacturer contains "Lenovo"
```

21. Make it case-sensitive using contains

A lot of operators that are by default case insensitive can become case-sensitive by adding a specific option **_cs** (cs for case sensitive). To make contains case sensitive, the operator to use is **contains_cs**.

```
Devices | where manufacturer contains_cs "Lenovo"
```

22. Display records where manufacturer contains leno using contains

The contains operator is used to filter results where a string exists. We have previously done the same filtering on lenovo word. Given that in "lenovo", there is the word "leno", the result will be the same.

```
Devices | where manufacturer contains "leno"
```

23. Display records where manufacturer is Lenovo using has

We have seen previously how to use the has operator.
The KQL query for our need will be:

```
Devices | where manufacturer has "lenovo"
```

See below the result:

username	device	manufacturer	model	SN
> luca	LENO_TST2	Lenovo	T14s	
> kevin	LENO_TST3	lenovo	T14s	TERY67

24. Display records where manufacturer is "dell" or "Lenovo" using has_any

We have seen previously how to use the **has_any** operator. The KQL query for our need will be:

```
Devices | where manufacturer has_any ("lenovo","dell")
```

25. Display records where manufacturer is lenovo using the in operator

Here we want to do the same than with the has operator but using in.

The is operator works as below:

```
Table | where ColumnName in (Pattern1, Pattern2,… )
```

The query for our example is:

```
Devices | where manufacturer in ("lenovo")
```

See below the result:

username	device	manufacturer	model	SN
> kevin	LENO_TST3	lenovo	T14s	TERY67

26. Display records where manufacturer is LENOVO using the in operator

Now let's use the same query but with the word lenovo with a L uppercase:

```
Devices | where manufacturer in ("Lenovo")
```

See below the result:

username	device	manufacturer	model	SN
> luca	LENO_TST2	Lenovo	T14s	

27. What did you notice?

By default, the in operator is case sensitive, meaning the result won't be the same if you type "lenovo" or "Lenovo" or "LENOVO".

28. Make it case insensitive

We have seen how to make contains case sensitive using **contains_cs**.
Here we want to do the opposite with in and make it case insensitive.
For that we will just add character "~" after the in operator like this **in~.**
The KQL query to get result for lenovo, Lenovo, LENOVO or any uppercase, lowercase string is:

```
Devices | where manufacturer in~ ("Lenovo")
```

It could be also:

```
Devices | where manufacturer in~ ("Lenovo")
Or
Devices | where manufacturer in~ ("lenovo")
Or
Devices | where manufacturer in~ ("LENOVO")
Or
Devices | where manufacturer in~ ("lenOVO")
```

The result will be the same and the following one:

username	device	manufacturer	model	SN
> luca	LENO_TST2	Lenovo	T14s	
> kevin	LENO_TST3	lenovo	T14s	TERY67

29. Display records where manufacturer is lenovo or dell using the in operator

The **in** operator to search for multiple patterns too, just like the has operator.
It will work as following: In the manufacturer column, show all records containing one of the following values: Value1, Value2, Value3.

The KQL query for lenovo or dell will be:

```
Devices | where manufacturer in ("lenovo", "dell")
```

See below the result:

username	device	manufacturer	model	SN
> kevin	LENO_TST3	lenovo	T14s	TERY67
> angel	TEST	dell	XPS 15	U8INYN

It's still case sensitive so we will need to add in~ to make it case insensitive:

```
Devices | where manufacturer in~ ("lenovo", "dell")
```

10. Display records where manufacturer contains "novo" using in and has operator

See below the query with in or has operators:

```
Devices | where manufacturer in ("novo")
Devices | where manufacturer has "novo"
```

See below the result:

11. What did you notice?

Result is empty because both has and in operators search for exact results meaning the column should contain exactly the string. In our example Manufacturer column contains the word novo but the whole string in the column is lenovo.

 DAY 7

2. Use the query 1, from the previous day
3. Display records not containing lenovo (not)

On the day 6, we have seen how to filter result on a specific string using the **has** or **contains** operator.
Now we need to do the same but where a string is not here.

You can do the opposite of a query easily by adding function **not()** as below:

```
Table | where not(your filter)
```

For instance, you have a filter **ColumnA contains MyString**, to get results where the column ColumnA have value MyString.
Using **not()**, you will get results where the column ColumnA does not have value MyString.

See below query we did on the previous day to get records containing "lenovo" using contains operator:

```
Devices | where data contains "lenovo"
```

To get opposite results meaning records without word "lenovo" we will add the **not** function as below:

```
Devices | where not (data contains "lenovo")
```

See below the result:

data
> {"username": "angel","device": "TEST","manufacturer": "dell","model":"XPS 15","SN":"U8INYN"}
> {"username": "mattias","device": "DELL1","manufacturer": "Dell","model":"XPS 13","SN":""}

4. Display records not containing dell or lenovo (not)

Here we want to filter on multiple strings with a OR.
We did this on the previous day to get result where data contain "dell" or "lenovo". See below the query we had:

```
Devices | where data has_any ("lenovo","dell")
```

Now we want the opposite, not "dell" or not "lenovo" using the not function.
See below the query:

```
Devices | where not(data has_any("lenovo", "dell"))
```

The result is empty because we don't have rows without "lenovo" or "dell", but if we replace "lenovo" with "Microsoft" it will show the row with "lenovo" but without "dell".

5. Display records not containing damien and lenovo (not)

We want now to do the same but with a AND instead of a OR.
See below the query we had on the previous day:

```
Devices | where data has_all ("lenovo","damien")
```

See below the opposite query with the not function:

```
Devices | where not(data has_all ("lenovo","damien"))
```

See below the result:

```
>    {"username": "luca","device": "LENO_TST3","manufacturer": "LENOVO","model":"T14s","SN":"TERY67"}
>    {"username": "angel","device": "TEST","manufacturer": "dell","model":"XPS 15","SN":"U8INYN"}
>    {"username": "mattias","device": "DELL1","manufacturer": "Dell","model":"XPS 13","SN":""}
```

6. Display records not containing lenovo (has or contains)

We have seen how to search if data not contains a specific string using the **not** function.
Some other operators allow you to do the same by adding character "**!**" before the operator.

See below some string operators with their opposite:

Exists operators	Not exist operators
Contains	!contains
Has	!has
In	!in
==	!=
Startswith	!startswith
Endswith	!endswith

See below query we did on the previous day to get records containing "lenovo" using **contains** operator:

```
Devices | where data contains "lenovo"
```

See below the opposite query:

```
Devices | where data !contains "lenovo"
```

See below the result:

> {"username": "angel","device": "TEST","manufacturer": "dell","model":"XPS 15","SN":"U8INYN"}

> {"username": "mattias","device": "DELL1","manufacturer": "Dell","model":"XPS 13","SN":""}

See below query we did on the previous day to get records containing "lenovo" using **has** operator:

```
Devices | where data has "lenovo"
```

See below the opposite query:

```
Devices | where data !has "lenovo"
```

See below the result:

> {"username": "angel","device": "TEST","manufacturer": "dell","model":"XPS 15","SN":"U8INYN"}

> {"username": "mattias","device": "DELL1","manufacturer": "Dell","model":"XPS 13","SN":""}

7. Use the query 15, from the previous day
8. Display records where manufacturer is not Lenovo (not, !contains, !has, !equals, !in)

On the previous day, we have seen how to use **has**, **contains** and **equals** operators. Let's do now the opposite queries.

See below the query using **has** and **!has**:

```
Devices | where manufacturer has "lenovo"
Devices | where manufacturer !has "lenovo"
```

See below the same using contains and !contains:

```
Devices | where manufacturer contains "lenovo"
Devices | where manufacturer !contains "lenovo"
```

See below the same using equals (==) and not equals (!=):

```
Devices | where manufacturer == "lenovo"
Devices | where manufacturer != "lenovo"
```

9. Display records where devicename starts with "leno"

To filter on a property starting with a specific string, the operator to use is **startswith** and works as below:

```
| where Column startswith "value"
```

In the following example, we will filter on the column manufacturer that should start with the string "leno":

```
Devices | where manufacturer startswith "leno"
```

You can do the same to search value ending with a specific string using the **endswith** operator. It works as below:

```
Devices | where manufacturer endswith "novo"
```

10. Display records where SN is not empty or null

It can be useful in KQL to filter on a column that should contain something, meaning it should not be empty.
The first way to proceed is to check if the column contains something using the following operators **<>** or **!=** as below:
```
| where Column <> ""
```
Or
```
| where Column != ""
```
The KQL query in our example to filter on column SN is:

```
Devices | where manufacturer <> ""
```
Or
```
Devices | where manufacturer != ""
```

Another way to check if a column is not empty is to use the **isnotempty** operator. This one work as below:

```
| where isnotempty(Column)
```

The KQL query in our example to filter on column SN is:
```
Devices | where isnotempty(manufacturer)
```

11. Display records where SN is empty or null

As with the **isnotempty** operator, you can look for empty value with the **isempty** operator.

```
Devices | where isempty(manufacturer)
```

12. Display records where SN and username are not empty

To filter on two not empty columns we will use where operator with AND, as below:

```
Devices
| where isnotempty(SN) or isnotempty(username)
```

 DAY 8

Demo lab environment

2. Use the following datatable
3. Filter on devices where both StorageTotal and StorageFree are not empty or null

As we have seen on day 7, to filter on result not empty or null we will use **isnotempty** and **isnotnull** operators:

```
| where isnotempty(StorageFree) and isnotempty(StorageTotal)
| where isnotnull(StorageFree) and isnotnull(StorageTotal)
```

4. Add two columns StorageTotalGB, StorageFreeGB with previous size converted to GB

Here we want to create a new column and calculate value.
To do that, we will use the **extend** operator, which allows you to create custom calculated columns and append them to the result set. It can be used as below:

```
| extend ColumnName == Value
```

Both StorageTotal and StorageFree values are in bytes.
To convert both StorageTotal and StorageFree values, we will divide value to 1024 as below:

```
StorageTotal /1024, StorageFreeGB = StorageFree /1024
```

The new created column using the **extend** operator will be as below:

```
| extend StorageTotalGB = StorageTotal /1024, StorageFreeGB
= StorageFree /1024
```

5. Calculate the used size on disk in a new column UsedSize

Now we want to calculate the used size meaning:
total size – free size ➜ StorageTotal – StorageFree.

We will use the **extend** operator just like before:

```
| extend UsedSize=StorageTotal - StorageFree
```

See below the result:

username	device	StorageFree	StorageTotal	UsedSize
> luca	DEVICE1	30494	242196	211702
> damien	DEVICE2	119382	242533	123151
> angel	DEVICE3	187654	242533	54879
> mattias	DESKTOP6-RRT	50352	242165	191813
> nicklas	TEST1	21038	242181	221143
> stephen	TEST2	29123	242921	213798

6. Convert UsedSize to GB

We have calculated the used size in the previous result.
To convert to GB, we will proceed as below:

```
| extend UsedSize=(StorageTotal - StorageFree) /1024
```

See below the result:

username	device	StorageFree	StorageTotal	UsedSize
> luca	DEVICE1	30494	242196	206
> damien	DEVICE2	119382	242533	120
> angel	DEVICE3	187654	242533	53
> mattias	DESKTOP6-RRT	50352	242165	187
> nicklas	TEST1	21038	242181	215
> stephen	TEST2	29123	242921	208

7. Add a column FreePercent with the free disk size percentage

To calculate the percentage of free disk space we will divide the free disk size with the full disk size and multiply to 100 as below:
((StorageFree)/(StorageTotal) * 100)

We need first to convert both values to a real as below:

```
(toreal(StorageFree) / toreal(StorageTotal) * 100)
```

Then we will use the extend operator to create the new calculated.
See below the query:

```
| extend FreePercent = round(toreal(StorageFree) /
toreal(StorageTotal) * 100)
```

The result will be something as below:

FreePercent	username	device	StorageFree	StorageTotal	UsedSize
> 13	luca	DEVICE1	30494	242196	206
> 49	damien	DEVICE2	119382	242533	120
> 77	angel	DEVICE3	187654	242533	53
> 21	mattias	DESKTOP6-RRT	50352	242165	187
> 9	nicklas	TEST1	21038	242181	215
> 12	stephen	TEST2	29123	242921	208

The full KQL query is:

```
Devices
| extend UsedSize=(StorageTotal - StorageFree) /1024
| extend FreePercent = round(toreal(StorageFree) /
toreal(StorageTotal) * 100)
```

Intune environment

1. In the IntuneDevices log, keep the last record for all devices

As we have seen on the day 4, to keep only the last record for a device we will use **summarize** and **arg_max**, as below:

```
| summarize arg_max(TimeGenerated,*) by DeviceName
```

2. Filter on devices where both StorageTotal and StorageFree are not empty or null

As we have seen on day 6, to filter on result not empty or null we will use **isnotempty** and **isnotnull** operators:

```
| where isnotempty(StorageFree) and isnotempty(StorageTotal)
| where isnotnull(StorageFree) and isnotnull(StorageTotal)
```

3. Do the same than in demo lab part 2, 3, 4, 5
Add two columns StorageTotalGB,StorageFreeGB with size converted to GB

Here we want to create a new column and calculate value.
To do that, we will use the **extend** operator, which allows you to create custom calculated columns and append them to the result set. It can be used as below:

```
| extend ColumnName == Value
```

To convert both StorageTotal and StorageFree columns to GB, we will divide value to 1024 as below:

```
StorageTotal /1024, StorageFreeGB = StorageFree /1024
```

The new created column using the extend operator will be as below:

```
| extend StorageTotalGB = StorageTotal /1024, StorageFreeGB
= StorageFree /1024
```

Add a column UsedSize and display the used size on disk

Now we want to calculate the used size meaning total size – free size: StorageTotal – StorageFree.
We will use the **extend** operator just like before:

```
| extend UsedSize=StorageTotal - StorageFree
```

Convert the previous result to GB

We have calculated the used size in the previous result.
Both StorageTotal and StorageFree values are in bytes.
To convert to GB, we will proceed as below:

```
| extend UsedSize=(StorageTotal - StorageFree) /1024
```

Add a column FreePercent with the free disk size percentage

To calculate the percentage of free disk space we will divide the free disk size with the full disk size and multiply to 100 as below:
((StorageFree)/(StorageTotal) * 100)

We need first to convert both values to a real as below:

```
(toreal(StorageFree) / toreal(StorageTotal) * 100)
```

Then, the new created column will be the following:

```
| extend FreePercent = round(toreal(StorageFree) /
toreal(StorageTotal) * 100)
```

 DAY 9

Demo lab environment

2. Use the previous query to get FreePercent

The KQL query was the below one:

```
Devices
| extend UsedSize=(StorageTotal - StorageFree) /1024
| extend FreePercent = round(toreal(StorageFree) /
toreal(StorageTotal) * 100)
```

3. Sort result on the device name

We have seen how to filter result through the query editor by clicking on a column header. Now let's do this directly in the query.
For that, we can use both **order** or **sort** operators which work as below:

```
| order by ColumnName
| sort by ColumnName
```

In our case it will be:

```
| order by device
```

There are two orders way:
- desc (descending): from low to high
- asc (ascending): from high to low

By default, if you don't specify it, the default order will be **desc**, meaning high to low.

See below the KQL query:
```
Devices
| extend UsedSize=(StorageTotal - StorageFree) /1024
| extend FreePercent = round(toreal(StorageFree) /
toreal(StorageTotal) * 100)
| order by device
```

4. Sort result on the free disk space percentage

We have ordered result on device column, now let's do this on the new FreePercent column, as below:

```
| order by FreePercent
| sort by FreePercent
```

See below the query:

```
Devices
| extend UsedSize=(StorageTotal - StorageFree) /1024
| extend FreePercent = round(toreal(StorageFree) /
toreal(StorageTotal) * 100)
| order by FreePercent
```

See below the result:

username	device	FreePercent
> franck	MYCOMP	81
> angel	DEVICE3	77
> abdelkarim	LPTP-321	77
> evrard	SAMCRO	62
> myriam	DKTP-123	51
> damien	DEVICE2	49

To change order from lesser free disk percent to higher, we will just change the order from descending to ascending by adding:

```
| order by FreePercent asc
```

See below the result:

username	device	FreePercent
> christophe	HELLOWORLD	3
> nicklas	TEST1	9
> stephen	TEST2	12
> luca	DEVICE1	13
> mattias	DESKTOP6-RRT	21

5. Display randomly 5 devices where free disk space percentage is lesser than 50%

As we have seen on the day 4, you can display random results using the **limit** or **take** operators.

We first need to filter results where FreePercent is lesser than 50%.
For that we will proceed as below:

```
| where FreePercent < 50
```

Now to choose randomly 5 devices from the result, we will use the **take** operator as below:

```
Devices
| extend UsedSize=(StorageTotal - StorageFree) /1024
| extend FreePercent = round(toreal(StorageFree) /
toreal(StorageTotal) * 100)
| where FreePercent < 50
| take 5
```

See below the result:

username	device	FreePercent
> luca	DEVICE1	13
> damien	DEVICE2	49
> mattias	DESKTOP6-RRT	21
> nicklas	TEST1	9
> stephen	TEST2	12

6. Display top 5 devices with most free disk space percentage

Instead of displaying 5 devices randomly, we want to display the top 5 devices with greater free disk size percent.
For that, the operator to use is **top**. It can be useful in your query to display top results, like top 5 devices with low disk space, with most BSOD...
The top operator can be used as below:

```
| top count by Column
```

By default, the top operator displays results from the high to low. In the previous example, we filter on devices with free disk percent lesser than 50%.
Here we want to filter where free disk percent is greater than 50%, as below:

```
| where FreePercent > 50
```

Now to get the top 5 devices with high free disk size we will just add the top operator as below:

```
Devices
| extend UsedSize=(StorageTotal - StorageFree) /1024
| extend FreePercent = round(toreal(StorageFree) /
toreal(StorageTotal) * 100)
| where FreePercent > 50
| top 5
```

See below the result:

username	...	device	FreePercent
> angel		DEVICE3	77
> franck		MYCOMP	81
> evrard		SAMCRO	62
> myriam		DKTP-123	51
> abdelkarim		LPTP-321	77

Intune environment

1. Use the IntuneDevices log
2. Do the same than in demo lab env part 2, 3, 4, 5, 6

Use the previous query to get the free disk space percentage

Here is the previous query:

```
IntuneDevices
| summarize arg_max(TimeGenerated,*) by DeviceName
```

```
| extend FreePercent = round(toreal(StorageFree) /
toreal(StorageTotal) * 100)
```

Sort the result on the device name

We have seen how to filter result through the query editor by clicking on a column header. Now let's do this directly in the query.
We will use here the **order** or **sort** operator.
This can be used as below:

```
| order by Column
| sort by Column
```

In our case it will be:

```
| order by DeviceName
```

There are two orders way:
- desc (descending): from low to high
- asc (ascending): from high to low

By default, if you don't specify it, the default order will be **desc**, meaning high to low.

Sort the result on the free disk space percentage

We have ordered result on DeviceName, now let's do this on the new FreePercent column, as below:

```
| order by FreePercent
```

Display randomly 10 devices where free disk space percentage is lesser than 50%

As we have seen on the day 4, you can display random results using the **limit** or **take** operators.
We first need to filter results where FreePercent is lesser than 50%.
For that we will proceed as below:

```
IntuneDevices
| summarize arg_max(TimeGenerated,*) by DeviceName
```

```
| extend FreePercent = round(toreal(StorageFree) /
toreal(StorageTotal) * 100)
| where FreePercent < 50
```

Now to choose randomly 10 devices from the result, we will use the take operator as below:

```
IntuneDevices
| summarize arg_max(TimeGenerated,*) by DeviceName
| extend FreePercent = round(toreal(StorageFree) /
toreal(StorageTotal) * 100)
| where FreePercent < 50
| take 10
```

3. Display top 10 devices with most free disk space percentage

Instead of displaying 10 devices randomly, we want to display the top 10 devices with greater free disk size percent.
For that, the operator to use is **top**. It can be useful in your query to display top results, like top 10 devices with low disk space, with most BSOD...
The top operator can be used as below:

```
| top count by Column
```

By default, the top operator displays results from the high to low. The query to display top 10 devices with high free disk size percent will be:

```
IntuneDevices
| summarize arg_max(TimeGenerated,*) by DeviceName
| extend FreePercent = round(toreal(StorageFree) /
toreal(StorageTotal) * 100)
| top 10 by FreePercent desc
```

You can change the order result by adding two strings to the order operator:
- Ascending: ascending order meaning low to high
- Descending: descending order meaning high to low

By default, if you don't specify it, the default order will be desc, meaning high to low.

 # DAY 10

Demo lab environment

2. Use the previous query to get free disk percent
3. Display records where free disk percent is lesser than 20%

See below the query we had to get the free disk size percent:

```
Devices
| extend UsedSize=(StorageTotal - StorageFree) /1024
| extend FreePercent = round(toreal(StorageFree) /
toreal(StorageTotal) * 100)
```

Now let's filter on records where FreePercent is lesser than 20%:

```
Devices
| extend UsedSize=(StorageTotal - StorageFree) /1024
| extend FreePercent = round(toreal(StorageFree) /
toreal(StorageTotal) * 100)
| where FreePercent < 20
```

4. Display records count

The idea is to count number records where free disk percent is lesser than 20%.
To do this the operator to use is **count** and works as below:

```
Your query | count
```

The full query for our example will be:

```
Devices
| extend UsedSize=(StorageTotal - StorageFree) /1024
| extend FreePercent = round(toreal(StorageFree) /
toreal(StorageTotal) * 100)
| where FreePercent < 20
| count
```

5. Display devices count where free disk percent is lesser than or equals to 5%

Here we want to do the same than before but where FreePercent is lesser than or equals to 5%. We want here lesser or equals meaning "**<=**".
We will proceed as before:

```
Devices
| extend UsedSize=(StorageTotal - StorageFree) /1024
| extend FreePercent = round(toreal(StorageFree) /
toreal(StorageTotal) * 100)
| where FreePercent <= 20
| count
```

6. Display devices count where free disk percent is between 20% and 50%

Now let's count devices where FreePercent is between 20% and 50%.
We will use the **where** operator with **and**, as below:

```
| where FreePercent > 20 and FreePercent < 50
```

See below the full query:

```
Devices
| extend UsedSize=(StorageTotal - StorageFree) /1024
| extend FreePercent = round(toreal(StorageFree) /
toreal(StorageTotal) * 100)
| where FreePercent > 20 and FreePercent < 50
| count
```

7. Create different column as below:
- Less 5%
- Between 5% and 20%
- Between 20% and 50%
- Above 60%: percent > 60%

The first step before creating columns is to get the free disk percent:

```
Devices
| extend UsedSize=(StorageTotal - StorageFree) /1024
| extend FreePercent = round(toreal(StorageFree) /
toreal(StorageTotal) * 100)
```

We want now to create multiple columns depending on value of the FreePercent column.
To proceed, we will use the **countif()** function.

The **countif** operator allows you to count records where a column has a specific value, for instance I want to count number of records when the column X has the value A.

As mentioned on the MS docs, this function is used in conjunction with the summarize operator.

Using the **countif** function, you can easily count different number of records depending on column values.
The **countif** function works as below:

```
| summarize NewColumn=countif(Column = Value)
```

Here we want to count number of records on the FreePercent column as below (condition = column name where to add data):
- If FreePercent < 5% = Less 5%
- If FreePercent > 5% and < 20% = Less 5%
- If FreePercent > 20% < 50% = Between 20% and 50%
- If FreePercent > 60% = Less 5%

The KQL with countif will be:

```
| summarize ['Less 5%']=countif(FreePercent <= 5),
['Between 5% and 20%']=countif(FreePercent > 5 and
FreePercent < 20),
['Between 20% and 50%']=countif(FreePercent >= 20 and
FreePercent <= 50),
['Above 60 %']=countif(FreePercent >= 60)
```

The full query is:

```
Devices
| extend UsedSize=(StorageTotal - StorageFree) /1024
| extend FreePercent = round(toreal(StorageFree) /
toreal(StorageTotal) * 100)
| summarize ['Less 5%']=countif(FreePercent <= 5),
['Between 5% and 20%']=countif(FreePercent > 5 and
FreePercent < 20),
['Between 20% and 50%']=countif(FreePercent >= 20 and
FreePercent <= 50),
['Above 60 %']=countif(FreePercent >= 60)
```

The result will be as below:

Less 5%	Between 5% and 20%	Between 20% and 50%	Above 60 %
1	3	2	4

Results Chart

Intune environment

1. Use the IntuneDevices log
2. Use the previous query to get free disk percent
3. Do the same than in demo lab env part 2, 3, 4, 5

Display records where free disk percent is less than 20%

See below the query we have seen before to get the free disk size percent:

```
IntuneDevices
| summarize arg_max(TimeGenerated,*) by DeviceName
| extend FreePercent = round(toreal(StorageFree) /
toreal(StorageTotal) * 100)
| where FreePercent > 50
```

Now let's filter on records where FreePercent is lesser than 20%:

```
IntuneDevices
| summarize arg_max(TimeGenerated,*) by DeviceName
| extend FreePercent = round(toreal(StorageFree) /
toreal(StorageTotal) * 100)
| where FreePercent < 20
```

Display records count

The idea is to count number records. To do this the operator to use is count as below:

```
| count
```

The full query will be:

```
IntuneDevices
| summarize arg_max(TimeGenerated,*) by DeviceName
```

```
| extend FreePercent = round(toreal(StorageFree) /
toreal(StorageTotal) * 100)
| where FreePercent < 20
| count
```

Display devices count where free disk percent is lesser than or equals to 5%

Here we want to count number of records where FreePercent is lesser than or equals to 5%. We will proceed as before:

```
IntuneDevices
| summarize arg_max(TimeGenerated,*) by DeviceName
| extend FreePercent = round(toreal(StorageFree) /
toreal(StorageTotal) * 100)
| where FreePercent <= 5
| count
```

Display devices count where free disk percent is between 20% and 50%

Now let's count devices where FreePercent is between 20% and 50%. We will use the **where** operator with **and**, as below:

```
| where FreePercent > 20 and FreePercent < 50
```

Create counters in different column as below:
- Less 5%: free disk percent <5%
- Between 5% and 20%
- Between 20% and 50%
- Above 60%: percent > 60%

The first step before creating columns is to get the free disk percent:

```
IntuneDevices
| summarize arg_max(TimeGenerated,*) by DeviceName
| extend FreePercent = round(toreal(StorageFree) /
toreal(StorageTotal) * 100)
```

We want now to create multiple columns depending on value of the FreePercent column.
To proceed, we will use the **countif()** function.

The **countif** operator allows you to count records where a column has a specific value, for instance I want to count number of records when the column X has the value A.

Using the **countif** function, you can easily count different number of records depending on column values.
The **countif** function works as below:

```
| summarize NewColumn=countif(Column = Value)
```

Here we want to count number of records on the FreePercent column as below (condition = column name where to add data):
- If FreePercent < 5% = Less 5%
- If FreePercent > 5% and < 20% = Less 5%
- If FreePercent > 20% < 50% = Between 20% and 50%
- If FreePercent > 60% = Less 5%

The KQL with countif will be:

```
| summarize ['Less 5%']=countif(FreePercent <= 5),
['Between 5% and 20%']=countif(FreePercent > 5 and
FreePercent < 20),
['Between 20% and 50%']=countif(FreePercent >= 20 and
FreePercent <= 50),
['Above 60 %']=countif(FreePercent >= 60)
```

The full query is:

```
IntuneDevices
| where isnotnull(StorageFree) and isnotnull(StorageTotal)
| extend FreePercent = round(toreal(StorageFree) /
toreal(StorageTotal) * 100)
| summarize ['Less 5%']=countif(FreePercent <= 5),
['Between 5% and 20%']=countif(FreePercent > 5 and
FreePercent < 20),
['Between 20% and 50%']=countif(FreePercent >= 20 and
FreePercent <= 50),
['Above 60 %']=countif(FreePercent >= 60)
```

The result will be as below:

Less 5%	Between 5% and 20%	Between 20% and 50%	Above 60 %
> 242	628	1820	1690

 DAY 11

Demo lab environment

2. Use the following datatable
3. In a new column, DiskState, add text as below:
   - If FreePercent < 20% then DiskState="Low disk space"
   - Else DiskState="Disk space OK"

On the last day we have seen how to use the **countif()** function to add some counters and count number of records depending on a condition in a column. Now instead of displaying just a count of devices, we want to add a new column with a specific text depending on the value in a column.

Here we want to create a column DiskState, then depending of the value of the FreePercent column, we want to change text in DiskState.
As you can see in the key words, there is an **iff** or **iif** function.
If you're familiar with PowerShell or some other language, you probably know the famous If, elseif, else.
The **iff** or **iif** KQL function does the same and works as below:

```
iff(if, then, else) or iif(if, then, else)
```

See below condition we want:
- If FreePercent < 20 then DiskState="Low disk space"
- Else DiskState="Disk space OK"

The **iff** function will be the following one:

```
| extend DiskState = iff(FreePercent < 20,"Low disk
space","Diskspace OK")
```

The full query is:

```
Devices
| extend FreePercent = round(toreal(StorageFree) /
toreal(StorageTotal) * 100)
| extend DiskState = iff(FreePercent < 20,"Low disk
space","Diskspace OK")
| project device,username,FreePercent,DiskState
```

See below the result:

device	username	FreePercent	DiskState
> DEVICE1	luca	13	Low disk space
> DEVICE2	damien	49	Diskspace OK
> DEVICE3	angel	77	Diskspace OK
> DESKTOP6-RRT	mattias	21	Diskspace OK
> TEST1	nicklas	9	Low disk space

4. Filter records where DiskState = "Low disk space"

We want now to display records where column DiskState equals Low Disk space. The filter to add to our query will be:

```
| where DiskState == "Low disk space"
```

5. Filter on records where actions are wipe or delete or remediation scripts and add value in a new column

Here we will create a new column ActionType in which we will add the value wipe or delete depending of the value of the Action column.
We will use the **extend** operator to add the column.
We will then use the **iif** function to get records depending on the value from the Action column:

See below our query:

```
Devices | extend ActionType = iff(Action contains "wipe", "wipe","delete")
```

See below the result:

device	username	Action	...	ActionType
> DEVICE1	luca	wipe device		wipe
> DEVICE2	damien	wipe device		wipe
> DEVICE3	angel	delete device		delete
> DESKTOP6-RRT	mattias	wipe script		wipe
> TEST1	nicklas	delete device		delete
> TEST2	stephen	delete script		delete

Intune environment

1. In IntuneDevices, use previous query to get free disk percent

The KQL query is the following one:

```
IntuneDevices
| where OS=="Windows"
| summarize arg_max(TimeGenerated,*) by DeviceName
| where isnotnull(StorageFree) and isnotnull(StorageTotal)
| extend FreePercent = round(toreal(StorageFree) /
toreal(StorageTotal) * 100)
```

2. Do the same than in demo lab env part 2, 3

Create a new column, DiskState, in which we will use a special function to get below results:
- If FreePercent < 20% then DiskState="Low disk space"
- Else DiskState="Disk space OK"

On the last day we have seen how to use the **countif** function to add some counters and count number of records depending on a condition in a column.

Now instead of displaying just a count of devices, we want to add a new column with a specific text depending on the value in a column.

Here we want to create a column DiskState. Depending of the value of the FreePercent column, we want to change text in DiskState.

As you can see in the key words, there is an **iff** or **iif** function. If you're familiar with PowerShell or some other language, you probably know the famous If, elseif, else.
The **iff** or **iif** KQL function does the same and works as below:

```
iff(if, then, else) or iif(if, then, else)
```

See below condition we want:
- If FreePercent < 20 then DiskState="Low disk space"
- Else DiskState="Disk space OK"

The **iff** function will be the following one:

```
| extend DiskState = iff(FreePercent < 20,"Low disk
space","Diskspace OK")
```

The full query is:

```
IntuneDevices
| where OS=="Windows"
| summarize arg_max(TimeGenerated,*) by DeviceName
| where isnotnull(StorageFree) and isnotnull(StorageTotal)
| extend FreePercent = round(toreal(StorageFree) /
toreal(StorageTotal) * 100)
| extend DiskState = iff(FreePercent < 20,"Low disk
space","Diskspace OK")
```

Filter now on records where column DiskState equals to "Low disk space"

We want now to display records where column DiskState equals Low Disk space. The KQL query will be:

```
IntuneDevices
| where OS=="Windows"
| summarize arg_max(TimeGenerated,*) by DeviceName
| where isnotnull(StorageFree) and isnotnull(StorageTotal)
| extend FreePercent = round(toreal(StorageFree) /
toreal(StorageTotal) * 100)
| extend DiskState = iff(FreePercent < 20,"Low disk
space","Diskspace OK")
| where DiskState == "Low disk space"
```

 DAY 12

Demo lab environment

2. In a new query create a variable A with value 5

To create a variable in KQL, we need to use the **let** statement.
It allows you to create a variable and add a value.
The let statement works as below:

```
let MyVariable = Value;
```

Don't forget the ; at the end of the query.

In our example the query is:

```
let a=5;
```

3. Display the content of the variable A

If you just type the name of the variable as below, you will have
an error:

```
let a=5;
a
```

To display the content of a variable we will use the **print**
operator as below:

```
let a=5;
print a
```

4. Now, create a variable A with value 10, and B with value 5
    and multiply both

We will first create both a and b variables with a let statement:

```
let a = 10;
let b = 5;
```

Next step is to use the print operator to multiply both variables:
```
print a*b
```

5. Use the datatable from the day 8 part 1

See below the query:

```
let Devices=datatable
(username:string,device:string,StorageFree:long,StorageTotal:long)
[
        "luca","DEVICE1","30494","242196",
        "damien","DEVICE2","119382","242533",
        "angel","DEVICE3","187654","242533",
        "mattias","DESKTOP6-RRT","50352","242165",
        "nicklas","TEST1","21038","242181",
        "stephen","TEST2","29123","242921",
        "franck","MYCOMP","196123","242533",
        "christophe","HELLOWORLD","7859","242551",
        "jax","SAMCRO","149965","241921"
];
```

6. Using the query to get FreePercent, create variable RequiredFreeSpace with value 30 and display devices where FreePercent is lesser than the RequiredFreeSpace

The first step is to set the RequiredFreeSpace in a variable as below:

```
let RequiredFreeSpace=30;
```

The next step is to add the FreePercent query we have seen. The last step is to filter results on records with FreePercent < 30. See below the full query:

```
let RequiredFreeSpace=30;
Devices
| extend FreePercent = round(toreal(StorageFree) /
toreal(StorageTotal) * 100)
| where FreePercent < RequiredFreeSpace
```

Intune environment

1. Do the same than in demo lab env part 1, 2, 3, 4

In a new query, create a variable a where value is 10, then a variable b where value is 5

To create a variable in KQL, we need to use the **let** statement.

It allows you to create a variable and add a value.
The let statement works as below:

```
let MyVariable = Value;
```

Don't forget the ; at the end of the query.

In our example the query is:

```
let a=5;
```

Display the content of the variable a

If you just type the name of the variable as below, you will have an error:

```
let a=5;
a
```

To display the content of a variable we will use the **print** operator as below:

```
let a=5;
print a
```

Create a variable A with value 10, and B with value 5 and multiply both

We will first create both a and b variables with a let statement:

```
let a = 10;
let b = 5;
```

Next step is to use the print operator to multiply both variables:

```
print a*b
```

1. In the IntuneDevices log, create a variable RequiredFreeSpace where value is 30

```
let RequiredFreeSpace=30;
```

2. Using the query to get the free disk space percent, display devices where percent is lesser than the variable RequiredFreeSpace

The first step is to set the RequiredFreeSpace in a variable as below:

```
let RequiredFreeSpace=30;
```

The next step is to add the FreePercent query we have seen. The last step is to filter results on records with FreePercent < 30. See below the full query:

```
let RequiredFreeSpace=30;
IntuneDevices
| summarize arg_max(TimeGenerated,*) by DeviceName
| where isnotnull(StorageFree) and isnotnull(StorageTotal)
| extend FreePercent = round(toreal(StorageFree) /
toreal(StorageTotal) * 100)
| where FreePercent < RequiredFreeSpace
```

Demo lab environment

2. Use the below datatable
3. Display records where LastContact column is < than 7 days

As we have seen on the day 2, to get records depending of a date you can use the **ago** function by specifying the number of days, hours...
Here the requested KQL query is:

```
Devices | where LastContact > ago(7d)
```

After running the query, the following error occurs:

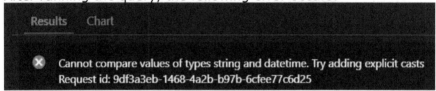

4. Why is there an error?

The message in the error is clear enough. It tells you that a string cannot be compared to a datetime.

It means that we're trying to compare a string to a datetime (trough the **ago** function).
We need first to convert the string to a datetime format.

5. Convert the LastContact column to a date

To convert a string to a date, datetime format, we need to use the **make_datetime** function.
This one allows you to create a datetime or convert an existing value to a date.
It can be used as below:

```
make_datetime(Value to convert)
```

Here we want to convert the LastContact column, so the KQL query will be:

```
make_datetime(LastContact)
```

We need then to add this in a new column using the extend operator:

```
| extend DeviceLastContact = make_datetime(LastContact)
```

See below the result:

username	device	LastContact	...	DeviceLastContact [UTC] ↑↓
> angel	DEVICE3	2024-10-04 22:02:42.0000000		10/4/2024, 10:02:42.000 PM
> nicklas	TEST1	2024-10-01 21:53:42.0000000		10/1/2024, 9:53:42.000 PM
> damien	DEVICE2	2024-09-29 21:36:42.0000000		9/29/2024, 9:36:42.000 PM
> luca	DEVICE1	2024-06-29 22:03:42.0000000		6/29/2024, 10:03:42.000 PM
> mattias	DESKTOP6-RRT	2023-05-01 22:00:42.0000000		5/1/2023, 10:00:42.000 PM

6. Display again records where LastContact is < than 7 days

We just converted the date in string to a date format.
Now we can use the ago() function to get records during the last 7 days, as below:

```
Devices
| extend DeviceLastContact= make_datetime(LastContact)
| where DeviceLastContact > ago(7d)
```

See below the result:

username	device	LastContact	DeviceLastContact [UTC] ↑↓
> angel	DEVICE3	2024-10-04 22:02:42.0000000	10/4/2024, 10:02:42.000 PM
> nicklas	TEST1	2024-10-01 21:53:42.0000000	10/1/2024, 9:53:42.000 PM
> damien	DEVICE2	2024-09-29 21:36:42.0000000	9/29/2024, 9:36:42.000 PM

7. Format the date as: MM/dd/yyyy

The previous query returns date from the DeviceLastContact column in the following format: 1/17/2024, 2:30:10.963 AM.

To change the format of the date, we can use the **format_datetime** function and specify the expected format. This function works as below:

```
format_datetime(Date,ExpectedFormat)
```

- The Date value is a datetime value
- The ExpectedFormat is a string

Here we want the date in the following format: Month/Day/Year. The ExpectedFormat string will be then: MM-dd-yyyy. See below the KQL query:

```
| extend DateFormat = format_datetime(DeviceLastContact,"MM-dd-yyyy")
```

See below the result:

username	device	LastContact	DeviceLastContact [UTC] ↑↓	DateFormat
> angel	DEVICE3	2024-10-04 22:02:42.0000000	10/4/2024, 10:02:42.000 PM	10-04-2024
> nicklas	TEST1	2024-10-01 21:53:42.0000000	10/1/2024, 9:53:42.000 PM	10-01-2024
> damien	DEVICE2	2024-09-29 21:36:42.0000000	9/29/2024, 9:36:42.000 PM	09-29-2024
> luca	DEVICE1	2024-06-29 22:03:42.0000000	6/29/2024, 10:03:42.000 PM	06-29-2024
> mattias	DESKTOP6...	2023-05-01 22:00:42.0000000	5/1/2023, 10:00:42.000 PM	05-01-2023

See below some examples of other formats you can use:

Format	Result
MM-dd-yyyy	01-17-2024
MM-dd-yy	01-17-24
yyyy-MM-dd	2024-01-17
MM-dd-yy [HH:mm:ss]	01-17-24 [02:30:18]
MM-dd-yy HH:mm:ss	01-17-24 02:30:18
MM-dd-yy HH:mm	01-17-24 02:30
MM-dd-yy [HH:mm:ss tt]	01-17-24 [02:30:18 AM]

See below the full KQL query:

```
Devices
| extend DeviceLastContact= make_datetime(LastContact)
| where DeviceLastContact > ago(7d)
| extend DateFormat = format_datetime(DeviceLastContact,"MM-dd-yyyy")
| project
username,device,LastContact,DeviceLastContact,DateFormat
```

8. Create a variable Date = '2023-12-18'

As we have seen on the previous day, in KQL we can create variable using the let statement.
See below the variable we want:

```
let Date = '2023-12-18'
```

9. In a new variable DateFormat, convert variable to a date

As before we will use the **make_datetime** function to convert the variable to a datetime format, as below:

```
| extend DateFormat = make_datetime(Date)
```

You can also use datetime function as below:

```
let Date_Format = datetime('2023-12-18');
```

10. In a new variable, Today, add the date of today

The first step to create the variable is to use the let statement. To get the date of today, meaning the date of now, the current time when you're trying the query, you can use the **now()** function. This one returns the current UTC time.
The variable will be:

```
let Today=now();
print Today
```

Result is the following one: 1/17/2024, 8:02:23.746 AM

11. Format the date as: month/day/year

We will use **format_datetime** to change the format of the date.
See below the KQL query:

```
let Today=now();
let DateFormat = format_datetime(Today,"MM-dd-yyyy");
```

See below the full KQL query:
```
let Today=now();
let DateFormat = format_datetime(Today,"MM-dd-yyyy");
print Today, DateFormat
```

12. Add 6 hours to the variable Today

The goal here is to add 6 hours to the current datetime. For instance, current time is 6AM, we want a new column with the current hour + 6, meaning 12AM.
In which case it can be useful you may ask.

It can be useful for instance in the following use case:
- You're running a script in Azure Automation
- The script uses Graph API to get data from Intune
- The script then sends data to Log Analytics
- The script is scheduled every 6 hours
- With data in Log Analytics, you want to create a workbook
- You need two cards with last data refresh and next one

Here we have the variable Today containing the current time using the **now()** function.

To add hour, days... to this datetime, there are two ways (at least):
- Using datetime_add function
- Adding directly + 6 hours to Today

The **datetime_add** function calculates a new datetime from a specified period.
It works as below:

```
datetime_add(Period,Amount,DateToChange)
```

- Period: can be hours, days, month, year, quarter, week, minute, second, millisecond, microsecond, nanosecond.
- Amount: number linked to Period, for instance 6 hours, 3 days, 3 months...
- DateToChange: datetime on which you want to apply the amount of period.

Here values are as below:
- Period: hour
- Amount: 6
- DateToChange: Today

The KQL query is:

```
let NextTime=datetime_add('hour',6,make_datetime(Today));
```

The following one will add 2 days to the current date from the Today column:

```
let NextTime=datetime_add('days',2,make_datetime(Today));
```

The second solution is: DateToChange + Amount Period

In our case it will be:

```
let NextTime=Today + 6hours;
```

The full KQL query is:

```
let Today=now();
let DateFormat = format_datetime(Today,"MM-dd-yyyy");
let NextTime=datetime_add('hour',6,make_datetime(Today));
print Now=Today,Next=NextTime
```

Result is the following one:

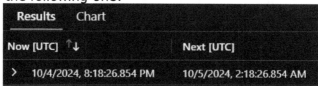

13. Format the variable Today to different time zone

We have created in the workbook, two cards to display the last data refresh and next one from the script.
The workbook should be available around the world, and you need to display the date in different timezone. We need to convert the now date to multiple time zone.

We have the previous query:

```
let today=now();
```

We will convert the date to the following timezone
- Date Pacific Standard Time
- Date Central Standard Time
- Date Central European Time

To convert a datetime to a specific timezone, we will use the **datetime_local_to_utc** function.

It can be used to convert local datetime to UTC datetime. This one work as below:

```
datetime_local_to_utc(DateToChange,Timezone)
```

See below how to write the timezone depending on our need:

- Date Pacific Standard Time: US/Pacific
- Date Central Standard Time: America/Chicago
- Date Central European Time: Europe/Paris

On the below link you can find all timezone available:
https://learn.microsoft.com/en-us/azure/data-explorer/kusto/query/timezone

See below the query to convert the date to the timezone:

```
datetime_local_to_utc(now(), "US/Pacific");
datetime_local_to_utc(now(), "America/Chicago");
datetime_local_to_utc(now(), "Europe/Paris");
```

See below the full query:

```
let ['Date Pacific Standard Time'] =
datetime_local_to_utc(now(), "US/Pacific");
let ['Date Central Standard Time'] =
datetime_local_to_utc(now(), "America/Chicago");
let ['Date Central European Time'] =
datetime_local_to_utc(now(), "Europe/Paris");
let today=now();
print today, ['Date Pacific Standard Time'],['Date Central
Standard Time'],['Date Central European Time']
```

See below the result:

Results	Chart		
print_0 [UTC] ↑↓	print_1 [UTC]	print_2 [UTC]	print_3 [UTC]
> 10/4/2024, 8:19:31.527 PM	10/5/2024, 3:19:31.527 AM	10/5/2024, 1:19:31.527 AM	10/4/2024, 6:19:31.527 PM

Intune environment

1. Use the IntuneDevices log
2. Do the same than in demo lab env part 2, 3, 4, 5, 6, 7, 8, 9, 10, 11

Display all records where the LastContact column is lesser than 7 days

As we have seen on the day 2, to get records depending of a date you can use the **ago** function by specifying the number of days, hours...
Here the requested KQL query is:

```
IntuneDevices
| where LastContact > ago(7d)
```

After running the query, the following error occurs:

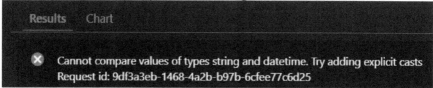

Why is there an error?

The message in the error is clear enough. It tells you that a string cannot be compared to a datetime.
At the beginning of the book, we have seen how to give a look to the structure of a log.
Let's check the IntuneDevices structure.
For that go to **Logs** > **LogManagement** > **IntuneDevices**:

You can see that the **lastContact** column is a **string**

```
𝑡 LastContact (string)
```

It means that we're trying to compare a string to a datetime (trough the **ago** function).
We need to convert the string to a datetime format.

Convert the LastContact column to a date

To convert a string to a date, datetime format, we need to use the **make_datetime** function.
This one allows you to create a datetime or convert an existing value to a date.
It can be used as below:

```
make_datetime(Value to convert)
```

Here we want to convert the LastContact column, so the KQL query will be:

```
make_datetime(LastContact)
```

We need then to add this in a new column using the extend operator:

```
| extend IntuneLastContact= make_datetime(LastContact)
```

Format the date as: MM/dd/yyyy

The previous query returns date from the IntuneLastContact column in the following format: 1/17/2024, 2:30:10.963 AM.

To change the format of the date, we can use the **format_datetime** function and specify the expected format.
This function works as below:

```
format_datetime(Date,ExpectedFormat)
```

- The Date value is a datetime value
- The ExpectedFormat is a string

Here we want the date in the following format: Month/Day/Year.
The ExpectedFormat string will be then: MM-dd-yyyy.

See below the KQL query:

```
| extend DateFormat = format_datetime(IntuneLastContact,"MM-
dd-yyyy")
```

In the below picture, I added a project to display both IntuneLastContact (before the format step) and DateFormat columns:

IntuneLastContact [UTC] ↑↓	DateFormat
> 2/3/2024, 2:29:27.345 AM	02-03-2024

See below some examples of other formats you can use:

Format	Result
MM-dd-yyyy	01-17-2024
MM-dd-yy	01-17-24
yyyy-MM-dd	2024-01-17
MM-dd-yy [HH:mm:ss]	01-17-24 [02:30:18]
MM-dd-yy HH:mm:ss	01-17-24 02:30:18
MM-dd-yy HH:mm	01-17-24 02:30
MM-dd-yy [HH:mm:ss tt]	01-17-24 [02:30:18 AM]

See below the full KQL query:

```
IntuneDevices
| summarize arg_max(TimeGenerated,*) by DeviceName
| extend IntuneLastContact= make_datetime(LastContact)
| where IntuneLastContact > ago(7d)
| extend DateFormat =
format_datetime(IntuneLastContact,"yyyy-MM-dd")
```

Create a variable Date = '2023-12-18'

As we have seen on the previous day, in KQL we can create variable using the let statement.
See below the variable we want:

```
let Date = '2023-12-18'
```

In a new variable DateFormat, convert variable to a date

As before we will use the **make_datetime** function to convert the variable to a datetime format, as below:

```
| extend DateFormat = make_datetime(Date)
```

You can also use datetime function as below:

```
let Date_Format = datetime('2023-12-18');
```

In a new variable, Today, add the date of today

The first step to create the variable is to use the let statement.
To get the date of today, meaning the date of now, the current
time when you're trying the query, you can use the now()
function.
This one returns the current UTC time.
The variable will be:

```
let Today=now();
print Today
```

Result is the following one: 1/17/2024, 8:02:23.746 AM

Format the date as: Month/Day/Year
We will use format_datetime to change the format of the date.
See below the KQL query:

```
let Today=now();
let DateFormat = format_datetime(Today,"MM-dd-yyyy");
```

See below the full KQL query:

```
let Today=now();
let DateFormat = format_datetime(Today,"MM-dd-yyyy");
print Today, DateFormat
```

Add 6 hours to the variable Today

The goal here is to add 6 hours to the current datetime. For
instance, current time is 6AM, we want a new column with the
current hour + 6, meaning 12AM.
In which case it can be useful you may ask.

It can be useful for instance in the following use case:
- You're running a script in Azure Automation
- The script uses Graph API to get data from Intune
- The script then sends data to Log Analytics

- The script is scheduled every 6 hours
- With data in Log Analytics, you want to create a workbook
- You need two cards with last data refresh and next one

Here we have the variable Today containing the current time using the **now()** function.

To add a hour, days... to this datetime, there are two ways (at least):
- Using datetime_add function
- Adding directly + 6 hours to Today

The **datetime_add** function calculates a new datetime from a specified period.
It works as below:

```
datetime_add(Period,Amount,DateToChange)
```

- Period: can be hours, days, month, year, quarter, week, minute, second, millisecond, microsecond, nanosecond.
- Amount: number linked to Period, for instance 6 hours, 3 days, 3 months...
- DateToChange: datetime on which you want to apply the amount of period.

Here values are as below:
- Period: hour
- Amount: 6
- DateToChange: Today

The KQL query is:

```
let NextTime=datetime_add('hour',6,make_datetime(Today));
```

The following one will add 2 days to the current date from the Today column:

```
let NextTime=datetime_add('days',2,make_datetime(Today));
```

The second solution is: DateToChange + Amount Period

In our case it will be:

```
let NextTime=Today + 6hours;
```

The full KQL query is:

```
let Today=now();
let DateFormat = format_datetime(Today,"MM-dd-yyyy");
let NextTime=datetime_add('hour',6,make_datetime(Today));
print Now=Today,Next=NextTime
```

Result is the following one:

Now [UTC] ↑↓	Next [UTC]
> 2/3/2024, 2:16:00.710 PM	2/3/2024, 8:16:00.710 PM

Format the variable Today to different time zone

We have created in the workbook, two cards to display the last data refresh and next one from the script.
The workbook should be available around the world, and you need to display the date in different timezone. We need to convert the now date to multiple time zone.

We have the previous query:

```
let today=now();
```

We will convert the date to the following timezone
- Date Pacific Standard Time
- Date Central Standard Time
- Date Central European Time

To convert a datetime to a specific timezone, we will use the **datetime_local_to_utc** function.

It can be used to convert local datetime to UTC datetime.
This one work as below:

```
datetime_local_to_utc(DateToChange,Timezone)
```

See below how to write the timezone depending on our need:

- Date Pacific Standard Time: US/Pacific
- Date Central Standard Time: America/Chicago
- Date Central European Time: Europe/Paris

On the below link you can find all timezone available:
https://learn.microsoft.com/en-us/azure/data-explorer/kusto/query/timezone

See below the query to convert the date to the timezone:

```
datetime_local_to_utc(now(), "US/Pacific");
datetime_local_to_utc(now(), "America/Chicago");
datetime_local_to_utc(now(), "Europe/Paris");
```

See below the full query:

```
let ['Date Pacific Standard Time'] =
datetime_local_to_utc(now(), "US/Pacific");
let ['Date Central Standard Time'] =
datetime_local_to_utc(now(), "America/Chicago");
let ['Date Central European Time'] =
datetime_local_to_utc(now(), "Europe/Paris");
print today, ['Date Pacific Standard Time'],['Date Central
Standard Time'],['Date Central European Time']
```

 DAY 14

2. Create a variable, Today, in which you add the date of today

As we have seen on the previous day we will use the **now()** function to get the current date and time.

```
Let Today=now();
```

3. Create a variable CustomDate with the following date value 2023-12-19 (in a date format of course)

As seen on the previous day, the KQL query is:

```
let CustomDate = '2023-12-18';
```

4. Create a variable DateDiff and calculate the difference between Today and CustomDate

Here we will just do a subtraction between both variables Today and CustomDate:

```
let Today = now();
let CustomDate_Format = datetime('2023-12-19');
let DateDiff = Today - CustomDate_Format;
print DateDiff
```

The result is the following:

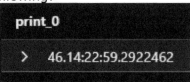

5. Convert the previous result to a number of days

If we give again a look to the previous date, we ca, notice that the date has some separator.
The date here is 30.20:05:54.8403976.

See below what contains the date after a subtraction:
- 30: number of days
- 20:05:54: 20hour 05 minutes 54 seconds

With KQL you can easily calculate the number of days, hours...
between two datetime values.
For that the function to use is **datetime_diff** and works as
below:

```
datetime_diff(Period,Date1,Date2)
```

- Period: can be Year, Quarter, Month, Week, Day, Hour,
  Minute, Second, Millisecond, Microsecond, Nanosecond
- Date1: datetime 1
- Date2: datetime 2

See below the appropriate query with our both variables Today
and CustomDate:

```
let TimeDiff = datetime_diff('day',Today,CustomDate_Format);
```

See below the full query:

```
let Today = now();
let CustomDate_Format = datetime('2023-12-19');
let TimeDiff = datetime_diff('day',Today,CustomDate_Format);
```

The result is: 30.

 DAY 15

Demo lab environment

2. Use the below datatable
3. Display records where last contact is between 5 and 9 days (different methods)

As we have seen on the day 12, the LastContact column is a string meaning we need to convert it to date.
We can do this using the below query:

```
| extend DeviceLastContact= make_datetime(LastContact)
```

Now we want to get value where this date is between two dates:
- < 5 days
- > 9 days

For that we have two ways:
- Using **where** and **ago**
- Using **between**

The first method is to filter on records using **where** operator as below:
- > 5 days: DeviceLastContact > ago(30d)
- < 9 days: DeviceLastContact < ago(7d)

If we check manually the data, we should have one entry between 5 and 9 days:
"damien","DEVICE2","2024-09-29 21:36:42 ","7859","242551",

The KQL query is:

```
Devices
| extend DeviceLastContact= make_datetime(LastContact)
| where DeviceLastContact < ago(5d) and DeviceLastContact > ago(9d)
```

See below the result:

device	...	username	DeviceLastContact [UTC] ↑
> DEVICE2		damien	9/29/2024, 9:36:42.000 PM

The other method is to use the **between** operator.

It can be used as below:

```
| where Column between (Date1 .. Date2)
```

The filter with **between** for our date is:

```
| where DeviceLastContact between (ago(9d) .. ago(5d))
```

The KQL query with **between** operator is:

```
Devices
| extend DeviceLastContact= make_datetime(LastContact)
| where DeviceLastContact between (ago(9d) .. ago(5d))
```

4. Display records where last contact is between today and 7 days

To get the date of today we will use the **now()** function, as we have seen before.
We will couple it with the **between** function as below:

```
Devices
| extend DeviceLastContact= make_datetime(LastContact)
| where DeviceLastContact between (ago(7d) .. now())
```

5. Calculate free disk percent and display devices where percent is between 0% and 5%

See below the query we have seen to get the free disk size percent:

```
Devices
| extend FreePercent = round(toreal(StorageFree) /
toreal(StorageTotal) * 100)
```

Now we want to filter on records where FreePercent is between 0% and 5%. We will use the between function as below:

```
| where FreePercent between (0 .. 5)
```

The full KQL query is:

```
Devices
| extend FreePercent = round(toreal(StorageFree) /
toreal(StorageTotal) * 100)
| where FreePercent between (0 .. 5)
```

See below the result:

device	username	FreePercent
> DEVICE1	luca	4
> DEVICE2	damien	3

Intune environment

Display records where last contact date is between 5 and 9 days (different methods)

As we have seen on the day 12, the LastContact column is a string meaning we need to convert it to date.
We can do this using the below query:

```
| extend Intunedate=make_datetime(LastContact)
```

Now we want to get value where this date, Intunedate, is between two dates:
- < 9 days
- > 5 days

For that we have two ways:
- Using **where** and **ago**
- Using **between**

The first method is to filter on records using **where** operator as below:
- < 9 days: Intunedate > ago(30d)
- > 5 days: Intunedate < ago(7d)

The KQL query is:
```
IntuneDevices
| extend Intunedate=make_datetime(LastContact)
| where Intunedate < ago(5d) and Intunedate > ago(9d)
```

The other method is to use the **between** operator.

It can be used as below:

```
| where Column between (Date1 .. Date2)
```

The KQL query with **between** operator is:

```
IntuneDevices
| extend Intunedate=make_datetime(LastContact)
| where Intunedate between (ago(9d) .. ago(5d))
```

Display records where last contact date is between now and 7 days

Let's use the previous between operator to do this. See below the appropriate query:

```
IntuneDevices
| extend Intunedate=make_datetime(LastContact)
| where Intunedate between (ago(7d) .. now())
```

Use the previous query to get the free disk space percent and display devices where percent is between 0% and 5%

See below the query we have seen to get the free disk size percent:

```
IntuneDevices
| summarize arg_max(TimeGenerated,*) by DeviceName
| extend FreePercent = round(toreal(StorageFree) /
toreal(StorageTotal) * 100)
```

Now we want to filter on records where FreePercent is between 0% and 5%. The KQL query is:

```
IntuneDevices
| summarize arg_max(TimeGenerated,*) by DeviceName
| extend FreePercent = round(toreal(StorageFree) /
toreal(StorageTotal) * 100)
| where FreePercent between (0 .. 5)
```

 DAY 16

2. Use the below query to create a specific table of data

```
datatable (Action:string)
[
"Executed by Damien Van Robaeys",
"Executed by Luca Van Robaeys"
]
```

3. Extract only the username, data after string Executed by

We have the following string "Executed by username".
We need to extract a specific part of this string.
For that we will use the **parse** operator that allows you to extract parts of a string from a specific pattern.
This one which works as below:

```
parse ColumnName with <Pattern> ExtractVariable
```

- ColumnName: name of the column where to extract data
- With: keyword to extract value with the parse operator
- Pattern: part allowing you to match a string

The **parse** operator will extract content located after the pattern **Pattern** in a new variable **ExtractVariable**.

See below the KQL query to extract username in a new column:

```
datatable (Action:string)
[
"Executed by Damien Van Robaeys",
"Executed by Luca Van Robaeys"
]
| parse Action with "Executed by " User | project User
```

See below the result:

Results	Chart

Action	User
> Executed by Damien Van Robaeys	Damien Van Robaeys
> Executed by Luca Van Robaeys	Luca Van Robaeys

---

4. Extract only the username, data after string "by"

In the above example we extracted content after exactly the pattern Executed by. Now we want to do the same by using only the keyword **by** instead of **Executed by**.
For that we will use the character *****, as below:

```
parse ColumnName with * <Pattern> ExtractVariable
```

See below the KQL query:

```
datatable (Action:string)
[
"Executed by Damien Van Robaeys",
"Executed by Luca Van Robaeys"
]
| parse Action with * "by" User
| project User
```

See below the result:

Results	Chart

User
> Damien Van Robaeys
> Luca Van Robaeys

5. Use the below query to create a specific table of data
```
datatable (Action:string)
[
"Program=Powershell;User=Damien Van Robaeys (DESKTOP-TST)",
"Program=python;User=Luca Van Robaeys (DESKTOP-TST2)",
]
```

6. Extract value after **Program** in a new a column **Program**

See below the result of the query we have:

Action
> Program=Powershell;User=Damien Van Robaeys (DESKTOP-TST)
> Program=python;User=Luca Van Robaeys (DESKTOP-TST2)

Now we want to get only the value after Program in a specific column.
We will use the parse function to extract this data and look into the Action column with the pattern Program.
See below the parse action:

```
| parse Action with "Program=" Program
```

The result is the following:

Program

> Powershell;User=Damien Van Robaeys (DESKTOP-TST)

> Powershell;User=Luca Van Robaeys (DESKTOP-TST)

As we only need the value after Program and not the part after, we will specify that the pattern is between **Program=** and ";".
See below the parse action:

```
| parse Action with "Program=" Program ";" *
```

See below the full KQL query:

```
datatable (Action:string)
[
"Program=Powershell;User=Damien Van Robaeys (DESKTOP-TST)",
"Program=Powershell;User=Luca Van Robaeys (DESKTOP-TST)",
]
| parse Action with "Program=" Program ";" *
| project Program
```

See below the result:

Results   Chart

Program

> Powershell

> Powershell

7. Extract both values **Program** and **User** in new columns

In the preview exercise we have extracted value after Program.
Now we need to the same with User meaning here we need to
extract multiple strings.
To extract multiple strings, we will proceed as below:

```
parse ColumnName with * Pattern1 ExtractVariable1 Pattern2
ExtractVariable2
```

We have previously extracted Program as below:

```
| parse Action with "Program=" Program ";" *
```

We will add the user extraction as below:

```
| parse Action with "Program=" Program ";" * 'User=' User
```

See below the full KQL query:

```
datatable (Action:string)
[
"Program=Powershell;User=Damien Van Robaeys (DESKTOP-TST)",
"Program=Powershell;User=Luca Van Robaeys (DESKTOP-TST)",
]
| parse Action with "Program=" Program ";" * 'User=' User
| project User,Program
```

See below the result:

Results	Chart	
User		**Program**
> Damien Van Robaeys (DESKTOP-TST)		Powershell
> Luca Van Robaeys (DESKTOP-TST)		Powershell

8. Create a variable to get the computer name between the "()"

In the previous example, we have a string like this for the User:
Luca Van Robaeys (DESKTOP-TST).
Now we only want the username and move the computer name
in a specific variable.

The first step is to change the User extraction to specify that the username is located between User= and character "(", as below:

```
| parse Action with "Program=" Program ";" * 'User=' User
"(" *
```

See below the result:

Results   Chart

User	Program
> Damien Van Robaeys	Powershell
> Luca Van Robaeys	Powershell

Now we want to add a ne variable to get the computer name that is between "(" and ")".
The equivalent parse is:

```
'(' Computer ")" //*
```

See below the full query:

```
datatable (Action:string)
[
"Program=Powershell;User=Damien Van Robaeys (DESKTOP-TST)",
"Program=Powershell;User=Luca Van Robaeys (DESKTOP-TST)",
]
| parse Action with "Program=" Program ";" * 'User=' User
'(' Computer ")" //*
| project Program,User,Computer
```

See below the result:

Program	User	Computer
> Powershell	Damien Van Robaeys	DESKTOP-TST
> Powershell	Luca Van Robaeys	DESKTOP-TST

9. In the SigninLogs log, use the in operator to filter on the following ResultType: 50126, 50133, 50144, 50133

To filter records as expected we will use the below query:

```
SigninLogs
| where ResultType in (50126,50133,50144,50133)
```

10. Using the parse operator, get the following information from the AuthenticationDetails column: authenticationMethod, authenticationStepDateTime

The idea now is to extract the following information from the AuthenticationDetails column: authenticationMethod, authentticationStepDateTime.

For that we will use the **parse** operator which works as below:

```
parse Column with * <regex1> variable <regex2> variable2
```

Here below is the KQL query example to extract the authenticationStepDateTime from the AuthenticationDetails column:

```
| parse AuthenticationDetails with *
'authenticationStepDateTime":"' AuthenticationDate '","' *
```

See below query to extract all columns we need:

```
| parse AuthenticationDetails with *
'authenticationStepDateTime":"' Date '","' *
'authenticationMethod":"' Method '","' *
```

See below the full query:

```
SigninLogs
| where ResultType in (50126,50133,50144,50133)
| parse AuthenticationDetails with *
'authenticationStepDateTime":"' Date '","' *
'authenticationMethod":"' Method '","' *
| project ResultType,ResultDescription,Date,Method
```

See below existing parse functions and what they do:
- parse_json: interprets a string as a JSON value and returns the value as dynamic

- parse_csv: splits a string representing a single record of comma-separated values and returns a string array with these values

- parse_command_line: parses a Unicode command-line string and returns a dynamic array of the command-line arguments
- parse_ipv4: converts IPv4 string to a signed 64-bit wide long number representation in big-endian order
- parse_path: Parses a file path string and returns a dynamic object
- parse_url: parses an absolute URL string and returns a dynamic object contains URL parts
- parse_urlquery: returns a dynamic object that contains the query parameters
- parse_user_agent: interprets a user-agent string, which identifies the user's browser and provides certain system details to servers hosting the websites the user visits
- parse_version: converts a string to a comparable decimal number
- parse_xml: interprets a string as an XML value, converts the value to a JSON, and returns the value as dynamic

 DAY 17

2. Use the below query to create a specific datatable

```
datatable (Devices:string)
[
'{"username": "damien van robaeys","device":
"DESKTOP_TEST","manufacturer": "lenovo","model":"T480s"}',
'{"username": "luca van robaeys","Device":
"DESKTOP_TST2","manufacturer": "lenovo","model":"T14s
Gen4"}'
]
```

See below what the result of this query:

Devices
> {"username": "damien van robaeys","device": "DESKTOP_TEST","manufacturer": "lenovo","model":"T480s"}
> {"username": "luca van robaeys","Device": "DESKTOP_TST2","manufacturer": "lenovo","model":"T14s Gen4"}

3. Extract username, devicename, manufacturer and model in different columns

The above string is in JSON format.
Here we want to extract each info from the JSON into separate columns. For that we will use the **parse_json** function.
The previous variable created is a string.

The goal of the **parse_json** function is to interpret a string as a JSON value and returns the value as dynamic.

The idea is to convert the string to a JSON and just get properties we need from the JSON.
The **parse_json** function works as below:

```
| extend JSON_Content=parse_json(Column)
| extend Property1=JSON_Content.Property1
| extend Property2=JSON_Content.Property2
```

The parse_json function was previously called todynamic. Both functions still work, and have the same behavior meaning you can use parse_json as well as todynamic.

See below how to use todynamic:

```
| extend JSON_Content=todynamic(Column)
| extend Property2=JSON_Content.Property2
| extend Property2=JSON_Content.Property2
```

Here we need the following properties: username, Device, Manufacturer, and model.

The **parse_json** is now:

```
User=(parse_json(Devices).username),
Model=(parse_json(Devices).model),
Device=(parse_json(Devices).device),
Manufacturer=(parse_json(Devices).manufacturer)
```

The full query is:

```
| extend JSON_Content=parse_json(Devices)
| extend username=JSON_Content.username
| extend devicename=JSON_Content.device
| extend manufacturer =JSON_Content.manufacturer
| extend model =JSON_Content.model
| project username, devicename, manufacturer, model
```

See below the result :

Results   Chart

username	devicename	manufacturer	model
> damien van robaeys	DESKTOP_TEST	lenovo	T480s
> luca van robaeys		lenovo	T14s Gen4

4. In the SecurityEvent log parse the UserData in EventData column and extract following info in different columns: PolicyName and FilePath

The first step is to see what contains the EventData column. For that we will use the below query:

```
SecurityEvent
| project EventData
```

EventData

˅ <EventData xmlns="http://schemas.microsoft.com/win/2004/08/events/event"> <Data Name="SubjectUserSid">S-1-5-18</Data> <Data Name="SubjectUserName">JBOX10$</Data> <Data Name=

EventData

```
<EventData xmlns="http://schemas.microsoft.com/win/2004/08/events/event">
  <Data Name="SubjectUserSid">S-1-5-18</Data>
  <Data Name="SubjectUserName">JBOX10$</Data>
  <Data Name="SubjectDomainName">WORKGROUP</Data>
  <Data Name="SubjectLogonId">0x3e7</Data>
  <Data Name="ProviderName">Microsoft Software Key Storage Provider</Data>
  <Data Name="AlgorithmName">UNKNOWN</Data>
  <Data Name="KeyName">{0867F8AA-C76E-40EB-8698-9D9D71883776}</Data>
  <Data Name="KeyType">%%2499</Data>
  <Data Name="KeyFilePath">C:\ProgramData\Microsoft\Crypto\RSA\MachineKeys\533e94879ca60ef2e801924e2b36bb70_8f1cba2f-ae9c-4d24-8e41-e05441927166</Data>
  <Data Name="Operation">%%2458</Data>
  <Data Name="ReturnCode">0x0</Data>
</EventData>
```

As you may notice, there is a word xmlns, meaning format is XML.

In the previous example, we have seen how to parse JSON content.

Now, to parse XML content, the KQL function to use is **parse_xml**. It works as below:

```
| extend XML_Content=parse_xml(Column)
| extend Property1=XML_Content.Property1
| extend Property2=XML_Content.Property2
```

The KQL query for our need is:

```
SecurityEvent
| project EventData
| extend XML_Content=parse_xml(EventData)
| extend UserData_Value=XML_Content.UserData
| where isnotempty(UserData_Value)
| extend FilePath=UserData_Value.RuleAndFileData.FilePath
| extend
PolicyName=UserData_Value.RuleAndFileData.PolicyName
| project PolicyName,FilePath
```

See below the result:

	PolicyName	FilePath
>	EXE	%WINDIR%\MICROSOFT.NET\FRAMEWORK64\V4.0.30319\CSC.EXE
>	EXE	%WINDIR%\MICROSOFT.NET\FRAMEWORK64\V4.0.30319\CVTRES.EXE
>	EXE	%SYSTEM32%\WINDOWSPOWERSHELL\V1.0\POWERSHELL.EXE
>	EXE	%SYSTEM32%\CONHOST.EXE
>	EXE	%WINDIR%\MICROSOFT.NET\FRAMEWORK64\V4.0.30319\CSC.EXE
>	EXE	%WINDIR%\MICROSOFT.NET\FRAMEWORK64\V4.0.30319\CVTRES.EXE
>	EXE	%WINDIR%\MICROSOFT.NET\FRAMEWORK64\V4.0.30319\CSC.EXE
>	EXE	%WINDIR%\MICROSOFT.NET\FRAMEWORK64\V4.0.30319\CVTRES.EXE
>	EXE	%SYSTEM32%\WINDOWSPOWERSHELL\V1.0\POWERSHELL.EXE

DAY 18

2. Use the below datatable
3. Filter on devices where version is 17.1.2 or something else

See below the query:

```
Devices
| where version =="17.1.2"
```

4. Filter now on version 17.1.2 or 16.5.1 or something else

You can do this using **where** operators or **in** as below:

```
| where version=="17.1.2" or version=="16.5.1"
```
Or
```
| where version in ("17.1.2","16.5.1")
```

5. Display records where version is lesser than 15.3.7 or something else

Basically, when you want to search data where something is lesser than something else you use the following structure:

```
| where value1 < value2
```

If you do this with the version field, you will have the below issue:

Results   Chart

 Cannot compare values of types string and string. Try adding explicit casts
Request id: 1df7db17-cbf8-49ae-a93b-92f7012d9173

It's because the version column is a string and cannot be compared to a version.

To manage version from string, you can use the **parse_version** function.
It allows you to convert the input string representation of the version to a comparable decimal number.

It works as below:

parse_version (StringToConvertToVersion)

To compare a string to another we can do this as below:

| where parse_version(String1) <= parse_version(String2)

The KQL query to compare the version column to a specific version is:

| where parse_version(version) <= parse_version("15.7.3")

 DAY 19

2. In a new query, create a variable var1 with value "hello"

As we have seen before, to create a variable we will use the let statement as below:

```
Let var1="hello";
```

3. Add a variable var2 with value "world"

```
Let var1="hello";
```

4. Concatenate both variables

To concatenate things with KQL, the function **strcat()** can be used.
It works as below:

```
strcat(argument1, argument2 [, argument3 ... ])
```

Here we want to concatenate var1 and var2 with a blank pace.
The KQL query is:

```
print strcat(var1," ",var2)
```

5. In a new query, create a variable longvalue with value 20L80004

```
let longvalue="20L80004324";
```

6. In a new variable shortvalue, split the variable longvalue to keep the last 4 characters

It can be useful to get only some characters from a string.
Here we have a string 20L80004324 and we need to keep only the first four characters.
We will use the substring function which allows you to extract a substring from the source string starting from some index to the end of the string.

The substring function works as below:

```
substring(SourceString, StartingIndex, Length)
```

- SourceString: the string you want to cut
- StartingIndex: character on which you want to start
- Length: length of characters to keep

Here we want to get the first four characters from the beginning of the string 20L80004324. It means we have the below conf:
- SourceString: 20L80004324
- StartingIndex: 0
- Length: 4

See below the KQL query:

```
substring(longvalue, 0, 4);
```

See below the full query:

```
let longvalue="20L80004324";
let shortvalue=substring(longvalue, 0, 4);
print longvalue,shortvalue
```

The result is: 20L8

If you want to keep the first four characters staring on the character L, the StartingIndex value will be 3.

7. In a new query add a variable user with the following email **damien.vanrobaeys@gmail.com**

```
let user = "damien.vanrobaeys@gmail.com";
```

8. In a new variable user_split, split the user variable to keep values before the @ character

Now we have a variable with an email address.
Here we want to get the part before the @, often firstname.lastname.
Another example is you have a product version like 7.1.3 and you want to only keep the major version meaning 7.
Both operations mentioned above are common tasks in programming stuff.

The term to do that is split meaning you want to split a string to keep a part of the string.
When you split the string **damien.vanrobaeys@gmail.com** on the @ character, you will get two strings, the one before the @ and the one after.

The split function in KQL works as below:

split(String,Delimiter)

- String: here it's damien.vanrobaeys@gmail.com
- Delimiter: here it's @

See below the KQL query:

```
let user = "damien.vanrobaeys@gmail.com";
let username = split(user,"@");
print username
```

This will separate result in two strings:
- damien
- vanrobaeys

To get one the two values, you need to specify its position.
It starts at position 0 meaning here position 0 is damien and position 1 is vanrobaeys.
See below how to specify the position:
- Username[0]: damien
- Username[1]: vanrobaeys

See below the KQL query to get only the part before the @, meaning position 0:

```
let user = "damien.vanrobaeys@gmail.com";
let user_split = split(user,"@");
let username = user_split[0];
print username
```

The split function can also be used as below:
split(String,Delimiter,Index)

- String: here it's damien.vanrobaeys@gmail.com
- Delimiter: here it's @
- Index: part to show before or after the delimiter

Here we want to show the part before the delimiter, before the @. The index to use is 0, as below:

```
split(user,"@",0)
```

See below the full query:

```
let user = "damien.vanrobaeys@gmail.com";
let username = split(user,"@",0);
print username
```

See below the result:

9. Create a variable with the following path
"C:\Users\damien.vanrobaeys\AppData\Local\Microsoft\Outlook"

To create the variable, we will use the **let** operator as below:

```
let test="C:\Users\damien\AppData\Local\Microsoft\Outlook";
```

10. Display content of the variable

When you run the above query, you will get the following error:

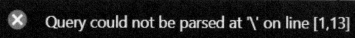

11. Why is there an error?

It's because of the \ character. You need to escape this one to use it.

12. Escape the \ character to display the variable

To escape the \ character, we just need to double it, meaning \ becomes ****.
See below the variable declaration:

```
let
test="C:\\Users\\damien\\AppData\\Local\\Microsoft\\Outlook"
;
```

13. Split the variable to show only the user name

We have seen previously how to use the split function.
Now we need to use it with the \ character.
See below how to use the split function with escaped \ character:

```
split(test,"\\")
```

Now we want to get only user name, meaning the 3rd part in our path.
See below how to get it with KQL:

```
let user=split(test,"\\",2)[0];
```

 DAY 20

Demo lab environment

2. Use the below datatable
3. Get the free disk percent

See below the appropriate query we have seen before:

```
Devices
| extend FreePercent = round(toreal(StorageFree) /
toreal(StorageTotal) * 100)
```

4. Depending on the percent create a new column DiskState and add text as below using the case function:
   - Above 5%: FreePercent < 5%
   - Between 5%-20%: FreePercent between 5% and 20%
   - Between 20%-50%: FreePercent between 20% and 50%
   - Above 50%: FreePercent greater than 50%

On the day 10, we have seen on to use the **iff** function to change value of column depending on a result of another value.
See below the query we used:

```
Devices
| extend FreePercent = round(toreal(StorageFree) /
toreal(StorageTotal) * 100)
| extend DiskSizeState = iff(FreePercent < 20,"Low disk
space","Diskspace OK")
```

Now we want to do approximatively the same but using the **case** function.
case is often used in programming like in PowerShell to evaluate something on do an action depending on the first value.
Here we want to create a new column DiskState and change its value depending on the FreePercent value.

The **case** function works as below:
```
case(Condition1,Action1,Condition2,Action2,…,else)
```

See below case for our example:

```
case(
FreePercent < 5, "Less 5%",
FreePercent >= 5 and FreePercent < 20, "Between 5% and 20%",
FreePercent >= 20 and FreePercent <= 50, "Between 20% and
50%",
FreePercent >= 50, "Above 50 %",
"Unknown")
```

See below the full query:

```
Devices
| extend FreePercent = round(toreal(StorageFree) /
toreal(StorageTotal) * 100)
| extend DiskState = case(
FreePercent < 5, "Less 5%",
FreePercent >= 5 and FreePercent < 20, "Between 5% and 20%",
FreePercent >= 20 and FreePercent <= 50, "Between 20% and
50%",
FreePercent >= 50, "Above 50 %",
"Unnown")
| project DeviceName,FreePercent,DiskState
```

See below the result:

device	FreePercent	DiskState
> DEVICE1	13	Between 5% and 20%
> DEVICE2	49	Between 20% and 50%
> DEVICE3	77	Above 50 %
> DESKTOP6-RRT	21	Between 20% and 50%
> TEST1	9	Between 5% and 20%

Intune environment

1. Use the IntuneDevices log and the query to get free disk percent

As we have seen before, the KQL query is:

```
IntuneDevices
| where OS=="Windows"
| where isnotnull(StorageFree) and isnotnull(StorageTotal)
| extend FreePercent = round(toreal(StorageFree) /
toreal(StorageTotal) * 100)
```

2. Depending on the percent create a new column DiskState and add text as below using the Case function:
    - Above 5%: FreePercent < 5%
    - Between 5%-20%: FreePercent between 5% and 20%
    - Between 20%-50%: FreePercent between 20% and 50%
    - Above 50%: FreePercent greater than 50%

On the day 10, we have seen on to use the iff function to change value of column depending on a result of another value.
See below the query we used:

```
IntuneDevices
| where OS=="Windows"
| summarize arg_max(TimeGenerated,*) by DeviceName
| where isnotnull(StorageFree) and isnotnull(StorageTotal)
| extend FreePercent = round(toreal(StorageFree) /
toreal(StorageTotal) * 100)
| extend DiskSizeState = iff(FreePercent < 20,"Low disk
space","Diskspace OK")
```

Now we want to do approximatively the same but using the **case** function.
Case is often used in programming like in PowerShell to evaluate something on do an action depending on the first value.

Here we want to create a new column DiskState and change its value depending on the FreePercent value.

The **case** function works as below:

```
case(Condition1,Action1,Condition2,Action2,…,else)
```

See below case for our example:

```
case(
FreePercent < 5, "Less 5%",
FreePercent >= 5 and FreePercent < 20, "Between 5% and 20%",
FreePercent >= 20 and FreePercent <= 50, "Between 20% and
50%",
FreePercent >= 50, "Above 50 %",
"Unknown")
```

See below the full query:

```
IntuneDevices
| where OS=="Windows"
| where isnotnull(StorageFree) and isnotnull(StorageTotal)
| extend FreePercent = round(toreal(StorageFree) /
toreal(StorageTotal) * 100)
| extend DiskState = case(
FreePercent < 5, "Less 5%",
FreePercent >= 5 and FreePercent < 20, "Between 5% and 20%",
FreePercent >= 20 and FreePercent <= 50, "Between 20% and
50%",
FreePercent >= 50, "Above 50 %",
"Unnown")
| project DeviceName,FreePercent,DiskState
```

DAY 21

2. Use the below datatable
3. In a new column MTM, split the Model column to keep only the first 4 characters

If you're familiar with Lenovo devices, the model returned in Intune is something like 20L8xxxx.
Lenovo devices return the MTM (Machine Type Model) as model instead of the friendly name which is not understandable in a report.
The MTM is composed of 4 characters, here the first four characters from the Model column.

Here we want to get the first four characters from the Model column.
We have previously seen that we can do this using the **substring** function.

Here below is the **substring** function to cut the Model column as expected (first four characaters):

```
Devices | extend MTM=substring(Model, 0, 4)
```

See below the result:

username	device	Model	MTM
> luca	DEVICE1	20NYSCP900	20NY
> damien	DEVICE2	20T1S20700	20T1
> angel	DEVICE3	20T1S20700	20T1
> mattias	DESKTOP6-RRT	20NYSCP900	20NY
> nicklas	TEST1	21BSS20L00	21BS
> stephen	TEST2	20L8S2AV00	20L8

We can see that in the MTM column value from the Model column has been shortened to keep the four first characters.

4. Add a new column FriendlyName in which replace the MTM with something more understandable as below:

- 20L8 with ThinkPad T480s
- 20T1 with ThinkPad T14s
- 20WN with ThinkPad T14s Gen2
- 21BS with ThinkPad T14s Gen3

Here we want to create a new column FriendlyName and add the real model for each Model.
In this column we want to replace the MTM value with the friendly name.

Replacing strings in KQL can be done using the **replace_string** function. It can be used to replaces all strings matches with specified strings.
The **replace_string** function works as below:

```
replace_string(Column,OldValue,NewValue)
```

Here is the KQL query to replace 20L8 with ThinkPad T480s:

```
replace_string(MTM,'20L8','ThinkPad T480s')
```

See below the full query:

```
Devices
| extend MTM=substring(Model, 0, 4)
| extend FriendlyName = replace_strings(
MTM,
dynamic(['20L8', '20T1','20WN','20NY','21BS']),
dynamic(['ThinkPad T480s', 'ThinkPad T14s','ThinkPad T14s
Gen2','T490s', "ThinkPad T14s Gen 3"]))
| project device,Model,MTM,FriendlyName
```

See below the result:

device	Model	MTM	FriendlyName
> DEVICE1	20NYSCP900	20NY	T490s
> DEVICE2	20T1S20700	20T1	ThinkPad T14s
> DEVICE3	20T1S20700	20T1	ThinkPad T14s
> DESKTOP6-RRT	20NYSCP900	20NY	T490s
> TEST1	21BSS20L00	21BS	ThinkPad T14s Gen 3
> TEST2	20L8S2AV00	20L8	ThinkPad T480s

 DAY 22

2. Use the following datatable
3. Count numbers of devices where model equals 20L8

As we have seen on the day 10, to count number of entries you just need to add **count** operator as below:

```
Your query | count
```

Here we want to count devices where model is 20L8 meaning we first need to filter on model as below:

```
Devices | where Model contains "20L8"
```

Now to do the count, we just need to add count operator:

```
Devices | where Model contains "20L8" | count
```

4. Count number of devices by model

In the previous example we used the **count** operator to count how many rows contain the string 20L8 in the Model column.
It will simply count number of records that are returned by the query.
The count operator can also be used to count records by something specific, meaning on a specific property like number of records by devices, by model, by user...

To count number of records on a specific column value we need to use both **summarize** operator with **count** function.
It will help you to count the number of records per summarization group. It works as below:

```
| summarize CountColumn=count() by PropertyToCount
```

- CountColumn: new column added with the count of records
- PropertyToCount: name of the column to count records

See below the full query:

```
Devices | summarize count() by Model
```

The result will be the following:

Model	count_
> 20NYSCP900	2
> 20T1S20700	3
> 21BSS20L00	1
> 20L8S2AV00	1
> 20WNS2UG00	1

As you may noticed, a new column **count_** is created with our count. To add the count in a specific column we will proceed as below:

```
| summarize DevicesCount = count() by Model
```

See below the result:

Model	DevicesCount
> 20NYSCP900	2
> 20T1S20700	3
> 21BSS20L00	1
> 20L8S2AV00	1
> 20WNS2UG00	1

5. Display the result in a Pie chart

When we run the previous query, it displays result in a Grid:

Model	DevicesCount
> 20NYSCP900	2
> 20T1S20700	3
> 21BSS20L00	1
> 20L8S2AV00	1
> 20WNS2UG00	1

Now we want to display result in a **Pie chart**.
To add a visual in a query, the query to use is **render**.

It wors as below:

```
| render visualization
```

Visualization can be:
anomalychart, areachart, barchart, piechart, card, columnchart, ladderchart, linechart, pivotchart, scatterchart, stackedareachart, table, timechart, timepivot, treemap

The full query will be:

```
Devices
| summarize count() by Model
| render piechart
```

See below the result:

See below an overview where render Visualization is barchart

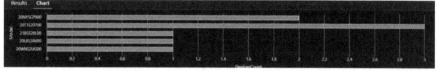

6. Sort order on devices count

Now we want to change the order of the result by displaying from the higher count to lesser. For that we will use the **order** operator, and set it on the DevicesCount column as below:

```
| order by DevicesCount
```

See below the result:

Model	DevicesCount
> 20T1S20700	3
> 20NYSCP900	2
> 21BSS20L00	1
> 20L8S2AV00	1
> 20WNS2UG00	1

7. Count the number of devices per user

On the previous query we did a count on Model.
Now we want to do the count on the user.
For that we will replace **Model** by **username** in the count, as below:

```
| summarize DevicesCount = count() by username
```

See below the result:

username	DevicesCount
> damien	2
> luca	2
> angel	1
> mattias	1
> christophe	1
> nicklas	1

We now have the number of devices per user.
Now to add a count on both models and users we need to add the username column to the count as below:

```
| summarize DevicesCount = count() by username, Model
```

8. Filter on user with more than 1 device

We now want to know users who have more than 1 device and number of devices for each of them.
We just need to use a where operator as below:

```
| where DevicesCount > 1
```

See below the full query:

```
Devices
| summarize DevicesCount = count() by username
| where DevicesCount > 1
| order by DevicesCount desc
```

 DAY 23

2. In a variable, devices, create a data table of values as below:
❖ Columns: devicename, username, manufacturer
❖ All columns are strings
▪ Row1: Computer1, damien.vanrobaeys, lenovo
▪ Row2: Computer2, luca.vanrobaeys, lenovo
▪ Row3: Computer3, walter.white, lenovo
▪ Row4: Computer1, jessie.pinkman, lenovo
▪ Display content of the variable devices

Here we want to create a table with data.
To do this with KQL, the operator to use is **datatable**.
It allows you to create a table of data defined in the query.
To create a datable the first step is to specify column headers and type, then values to add.
See below how to use the datable operator:

```
Datatable(Column1Name:Type, Column2Name:Type…)
[Data to add]
```

We will first specify columns name and type:

```
let Devices=datatable
(devicename:string,username:string,manufacturer:string)
```

See below the query:

```
let Devices=datatable
(devicename:string,username:string,manufacturer:string)
[
    "Computer1","damien.vanrobaeys","lenovo",
    "Computer2","luca.vanrobaeys","lenovo",
    "Computer3","walter.white","dell",
    "Computer4","jessie.pinkman","lenovo",
    "Computer5","gustavo.fringe","hp",
    "Computer6","tony.soprano","dell",
    "Computer7","jax.teller","lenovo",
];
Devices
```

See below the result:

devicename	username	manufacturer
> Computer1	damien.vanrobaeys	lenovo
> Computer2	luca.vanrobaeys	lenovo
> Computer3	walter.white	dell
> Computer4	jessie.pinkman	lenovo
> Computer5	gustavo.fringe	hp
> Computer6	tony.soprano	dell
> Computer7	jax.teller	lenovo

3. In a variable, BSOD, create a data table of values as below:
❖ Columns: devicename, BSODCount, BSODCode, Model, BIOSVersion
❖ All columns are strings except BSODCount which is an integer
- Row1: Computer1,4,0x000000A0, ThinkPad T480s,1.49
- Row2: Computer2,1,0x00000116, ThinkPad T14s,1.24
- Row3: Computer3,15,0x000000A0, ThinkPad T14s Gen2,1.50
- Row4: Computer4,0,0x00000154, ThinkPad T14s Gen3,1.50
- Row5: Computer5,2,0x00000154, ThinkPad T14s,1.24
- Row6: Computer6,5,0x00000154, ThinkPad T480s,1.49
- Row7: Computer7,10,0x00000154, ThinkPad T490s,1.49

As with the Devices table, we will create a new table of data using the **datatable** operator, as below:

```
let BSOD=datatable
(devicename:string,BSODCount:int,BSODCode:string,Model:strin
g,BIOSVersion:string)
[
"Computer1","4","0x000000A0","ThinkPad T480s","1.49",
"Computer2","1","0x00000116","ThinkPad T14s","1.24 ",
"Computer3","15","0x000000A0","ThinkPad T14s Gen2","1.50",
"Computer4","0","0x00000154","ThinkPad T14s Gen3","1.50",
];
```

See below the result:

devicename	BSODCount	BSODCode	Model	BIOSVersion
> Computer1	4	0x000000A0	ThinkPad T480s	1.49
> Computer2	1	0x00000116	ThinkPad T14s	1.24
> Computer3	15	0x000000A0	ThinkPad T14s Gen2	1.50
> Computer4	0	0x00000154	ThinkPad T14s Gen3	1.50

4. In the Devices table, filter on Lenovo devices

Here we want to filter records from the Devices table. We will proceed like basic table, log using a **where** operator.
See below the query:

```
Devices | where manufacturer contains "lenovo"
```

See below the result:

devicename	username	manufacturer
> Computer1	damien.vanrobaeys	lenovo
> Computer2	luca.vanrobaeys	lenovo
> Computer4	jessie.pinkman	lenovo
> Computer7	jax.teller	lenovo

5. In the BSOD log, filter on records with more than 5 BSOD

See below the query:

```
BSOD | where BSODCount > 5
```

See below the result:

devicename	BSODCount	BSODCode	Model	...	BIOSVersion
> Computer3	15	0x000000A0	ThinkPad T14s Gen2		1.50

 DAY 24

2. Use both previous devices and BSOD variables
3. What is common value between both tables?

See below the result from the table Devices:

devicename	username	manufacturer
> Computer1	damien.vanrobaeys	lenovo
> Computer2	luca.vanrobaeys	lenovo
> Computer3	walter.white	dell
> Computer4	jessie.pinkman	lenovo
> Computer5	gustavo.fringe	hp
> Computer6	tony.soprano	dell
> Computer7	jax.teller	lenovo

See below the result from the table BSOD:

devicename	BSODCount	BSODCode	Model	...	BIOSVersion
> Computer1	4	0x000000A0	ThinkPad T480s		1.49
> Computer2	1	0x00000116	ThinkPad T14s		1.24
> Computer3	15	0x000000A0	ThinkPad T14s Gen2		1.50
> Computer4	0	0x00000154	ThinkPad T14s Gen3		1.50

Both tables give different information but there is one common field, one common column, the column **devicename**.
This is the common id between both tables.

4. What is the column that you can use to join both tables?

The common id is devicename as it exists in both tables. The column that we can use to join both tables is devicename.

5. Join both devices and BSOD tables

The join operation allows you to join data from a table to another table. This way you can bind information from both columns.

Here the idea is to get BSOD information for a device from the column Devices.
To join a table to another table, the operator is easy to know because it speaks as itself, it's the **join** operator.

The **join** operator is used to merge rows of two tables to form a new table by matching values of the specified columns from each table.
It works as below:

```
Table1
| join Table2 on CommonID
```

Here the Table1 is Devices, Table2 is BSOD and CommonID is DeviceName, as below:

```
Devices
| join BSOD on devicename
```

The CommonID is used to join both tables because it's a field that has the same information, meaning we can find this id in both tables. It's used a lot in data base process.

Here is the default result after joining both tables:

devicename	username	manufacturer	devicename1	BSODCount	BSODCode	Model	BIOSVersion
Computer1	damien.vanrobaeys	lenovo	Computer1	4	0x000000A0	ThinkPad T480s	1.49
Computer2	luca.vanrobaeys	lenovo	Computer2	1	0x00000116	ThinkPad T14s	1.24
Computer3	walter.white	dell	Computer3	15	0x000000A0	ThinkPad T14s Gen2	1.50
Computer4	jessie.pinkman	lenovo	Computer4	0	0x00000154	ThinkPad T14s Gen3	1.50

6. What did you notice about the common field?

The common field, **devicename**, is duplicated, we have the devicename from the Devices table, on there is devicename1 from the BSOD table.

7. Remove the common column from the BSOD table

As we have seen at the beginning of the book, to choose which column to display or not, the operator to use is **project**.
Here we want to remove an existing column from the display. To do this we will use **project-away**, as below:

```
| project-away devicename1
```

8. Now use the following datatables
9. What did you notice between both tables?

Here we don't have a column with the same name in both tables. In this previous exercise we had the column devicename that was in both tables. It was the common column that we can used to join both tables.

10. Join both tables (two ways)

Even if we don't have a column with same name in both tables, we have a column with same information, the name of the computer.
While in the **BSOD** table we have a **device** column, in the **Devices** table we have a **computer** column. This is the column that we can use to join both tables. If we try to join both tables as previously, we will have an error:

```
Devices | join BSOD on device
```

> ⊗ 'join' operator: Failed to resolve scalar expression named 'device'
> Request id: 990aacd7-630f-4f87-b107-aea6831d55b7

This error is because it doesn't find a column device in the BSOD table. To join both tables we have two ways.

The first way is to use the **extend** operator to rename column computer from the Devices table to fit with column name from the BSOD table. The new name of the computer column should be device.
See below how to rename this column using extend:

```
| extend device=computer
```

See below the full join KQL query:

```
Devices
| extend device=computer
| join BSOD on device
```

See below the result:

computer	user	manufacturer	device	device1	BSODCount	BSODCode	Model
> Computer1	damien.vanrobaeys	lenovo	Computer1	Computer1	4	0x000000A0	ThinkPad T480s
> Computer2	luca.vanrobaeys	lenovo	Computer2	Computer2	1	0x00000116	ThinkPad T14s

The other way is to select which column to choose in both tables as following: we will join table **BSOD** from the **Devices** table where the column **device** from the right table is equal to the column **computer** from the left table.

Here we need to:
- specify name of the columns to use
- use equals operator "==" to show they match
- specify from which side of the query the columns come from

To specify the side of the data, we will use $left and $right before the column names.

The join query is the following one:

```
Table1
| join Table2 on $right.Table1Column == $left.Table2Comlumn
```

The query we used before is the following:

```
Devices
| join BSOD
```

It means we want to join the BSOD table from the Devices table. Here the first table, Devices, is the left side whereas the BSOD table (table we want to join is on the right side).

Here the query to join both tables without renaming a column is:

```
Devices
| join BSOD on $right.device == $left.computer
```

 DAY 25

2. Use the previous query with devices and BSOD tables
3. What did you notice in the fields from the devices table, after joining both tables?

The rows 5, 6 and 7 meaning Computer5, Computer6 and Computer7 are not displayed after joining both tables.

devicename	username	manufacturer	devicename1	BSODCount	BSODCode	Model	BIOSVersion
> Computer1	damien.vanrobaeys	lenovo	Computer1	4	0x000000A0	ThinkPad T480s	1.49
> Computer2	luca.vanrobaeys	lenovo	Computer2	1	0x00000116	ThinkPad T14s	1.24
> Computer3	walter.white	dell	Computer3	15	0x000000A0	ThinkPad T14s Gen2	1.50
> Computer4	jessie.pinkman	lenovo	Computer4	0	0x00000154	ThinkPad T14s Gen3	1.50

This is because of the join **kind**. By default, the join **kind** is **innerunique**.
Innerunique kind merges all deduplicated rows from the left table that match rows from the right table.
That's why the default join only rows 1, 2, 3 and 4 because Computer1, Computer2, Computer3 and Computer4 are available in both tables.

4. Change the join type using the kind attribute with inner and innerunique value

The kind can be configured as below:

```
Table1
| join kind=kind Table2
```

Let's change the kind from innerunique to inner, as below:

```
Devices
| join kind=inner BSOD on devicename
```

The inner kind will merge only matching rows from both tables. In our case, result is the same than innerunique.

5. Test other kind

See below different join kind:

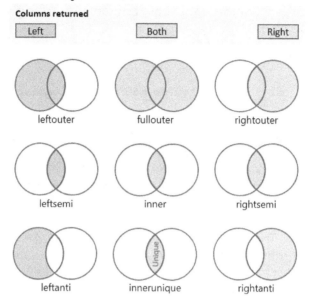

Leftouter kind
Merge properties
- All columns from both tables, including the matching keys
- All records from the left table and only matching rows from the right table

See below the query:

```
Devices | join kind=leftouter BSOD on devicename
```

See below the result:

As you may notice:
- All rows from the Devices table are displayed
- The common id, devicename, is duplicated

Rightouter kind
Merge properties
- All columns from both tables, including the matching keys
- All records from the right table and only matching rows from the left table

See below the query:

```
Devices | join kind=rightouter BSOD on devicename
```

See below the result:

devicename	username	manufacturer	devicename1	BSODCount	BSODCode	Model	BIOSVersion
> Computer1	damien.vanrobaeys	lenovo	Computer1	4	0x000000A0	ThinkPad T480s	1.49
> Computer2	luca.vanrobaeys	lenovo	Computer2	1	0x00000116	ThinkPad T14s	1.24
> Computer3	walter.white	dell	Computer3	15	0x000000A0	ThinkPad T14s Gen2	1.50
> Computer4	jessie.pinkman	lenovo	Computer4	0	0x00000154	ThinkPad T14s Gen3	1.50

As you may notice:
- Only rows from the Devices table are displayed
- The common id, devicename, is duplicated

Fullouter kind
Merge properties
- All columns from both tables, including the matching keys
- All records from both tables with unmatched cells populated with null

See below the query:

```
Devices | join kind=fullouter BSOD on devicename
```

See below the result:

devicename	username	manufacturer	devicename1	BSODCount	BSODCode	Model	BIOSVersion
> Computer1	damien.vanrobaeys	lenovo	Computer1	4	0x000000A0	ThinkPad T480s	1.49
> Computer2	luca.vanrobaeys	lenovo	Computer2	1	0x00000116	ThinkPad T14s	1.24
> Computer3	walter.white	dell	Computer3	15	0x000000A0	ThinkPad T14s Gen2	1.50
> Computer4	jessie.pinkman	lenovo	Computer4	0	0x00000154	ThinkPad T14s Gen3	1.50
> Computer5	gustavo.fringe	hp					
> Computer6	tony.soprano	dell					
> Computer7	jax.teller	lenovo					

As you may notice:
- All rows from the Devices table are displayed
- The common id, devicename, is duplicated

leftsemi kind
Merge properties
- All columns from the left table
- All records from the left table that match records from the right table

See below the query:

```
Devices | join kind=leftsemi BSOD on devicename
```

See below the result:

devicename	username	manufacturer
> Computer1	damien.vanrobaeys	lenovo
> Computer2	luca.vanrobaeys	lenovo
> Computer3	walter.white	dell
> Computer4	jessie.pinkman	lenovo

As you may notice:
- Only common rows from both tables are displayed
- Only columns from table Devices (left) are displayed

rightsemi kind
Merge properties
- All columns from the right table
- All records from the right table that match records from the left table

See below the query:

```
Devices | join kind=rightsemi BSOD on devicename
```

See below the result:

devicename	BSODCount	BSODCode	Model	...	BIOSVersion
> Computer1	4	0x000000A0	ThinkPad T480s		1.49
> Computer2	1	0x00000116	ThinkPad T14s		1.24
> Computer3	15	0x000000A0	ThinkPad T14s Gen2		1.50
> Computer4	0	0x00000154	ThinkPad T14s Gen3		1.50

As you may notice:
- Only common rows from both tables are displayed
- Only columns from table BSOD (right) are displayed

 DAY 26

2. Use the previous query with devices and BSOD tables

See below the query to join both tables:

```
Devices
| join (BSOD | where BSODCount > 5) on devicename
```

3. Join both devices and join tables only for devices with more than 5 BSOD

To filter records on a table, you need to use **where** operator. Filtering a table whole joining it can be did using the same way. See below how to join a table with another table depending on a condition:

```
Table1
| join (Table2 | where Condition) on CommonID
```

See below what we need:
-   Table1: Devices
-   Table2: BSOD
-   Condition: More than 5 BSOD
-   CommonID: devicename

See below the query:

```
Devices
| join (BSOD | where BSODCount > 5) on devicename
```

 DAY 27

2. Join both devices and BSOD tables using the union operator instead of the join operator

Another operator allows you to join different tables. This one is the **union** operator. It takes two or more tables and returns the rows of all of them.
It works as below:

```
Table1
| union Table2
```

In our example Table1 is Devices and Table2 is BSOD:

```
Devices
| union BSOD
```

See below the result:

devicename	username	manufactu...	BSODCount	BSODCode	Model	...	BIOSVersion
> Computer1	damien.vanrobaeys	lenovo					
> Computer2	luca.vanrobaeys	lenovo					
> Computer3	walter.white	dell					
> Computer4	jessie.pinkman	lenovo					
> Computer5	gustavo.fringe	hp					
> Computer6	tony.soprano	dell					
> Computer7	jax.teller	lenovo					
> Computer1			4	0x000000A0	ThinkPad T480s		1.49
> Computer2			1	0x00000116	ThinkPad T14s		1.24
> Computer3			15	0x000000A0	ThinkPad T14s Gen2		1.50
> Computer4			0	0x00000154	ThinkPad T14s Gen3		1.50

See below result from join operator:

devicename	username	manufacturer	devicename1	BSODCount	BSODCode	Model	BIOSVersion
> Computer1	damien.vanrobaeys	lenovo	Computer1	4	0x000000A0	ThinkPad T480s	1.49
> Computer2	luca.vanrobaeys	lenovo	Computer2	1	0x00000116	ThinkPad T14s	1.24
> Computer3	walter.white	dell	Computer3	15	0x000000A0	ThinkPad T14s Gen2	1.50
> Computer4	jessie.pinkman	lenovo	Computer4	0	0x00000154	ThinkPad T14s Gen3	1.50

3. What did you notice?

First in the query, no need to specify a common id.
Then in the result the union will show all rows from the table1 and all rows from the table2. It will also show all columns from both tables.

4. Join both devices and BSOD tables using the lookup operator instead of the join operator

Another operator allows you to join different tables.
This one is the **lookup** operator.

The lookup operator works like the join operator and performs an operation like the join operator with the following differences:
- The result doesn't repeat columns from the right table
- Two kinds of lookup: leftouter (default) and inner
- Assumes that the left table is the larger table, and the right table is the smaller table

It works as below:

Table1
| lookup Table2 on CommonID

In our example Table1 is Devices and Table2 is BSOD and CommonID is devicename.

Devices
| lookup BSOD on devicename

See below the result:

devicename	username	manufacturer	BSODCount	BSODCode	Model	...	BIOSVersion
> Computer1	damien.vanrobaeys	lenovo	4	0x000000A0	ThinkPad T480s		1.49
> Computer2	luca.vanrobaeys	lenovo	1	0x00000116	ThinkPad T14s		1.24
> Computer3	walter.white	dell	15	0x000000A0	ThinkPad T14s Gen2		1.50
> Computer4	jessie.pinkman	lenovo	0	0x00000154	ThinkPad T14s Gen3		1.50
> Computer5	gustavo.fringe	hp					
> Computer6	tony.soprano	dell					
> Computer7	jax.teller	lenovo					

See below result from join operator:

devicename	username	manufacturer	devicename1	BSODCount	BSODCode	Model	BIOSVersion
> Computer1	damien.vanrobaeys	lenovo	Computer1	4	0x000000A0	ThinkPad T480s	1.49
> Computer2	luca.vanrobaeys	lenovo	Computer2	1	0x00000116	ThinkPad T14s	1.24
> Computer3	walter.white	dell	Computer3	15	0x000000A0	ThinkPad T14s Gen2	1.50
> Computer4	jessie.pinkman	lenovo	Computer4	0	0x00000154	ThinkPad T14s Gen3	1.50

5. What did you notice?

All rows from both tables are displayed, here Computer1 to Computer7, whereas with the basic join only rows with a match n the second table.

It also displays all columns from both tables and there is no duplicated column like with the devicename1 with the join operation.

 DAY 28

2. In the following exercise you have two workspaces (test1 and test2)
3. From the workspace test1, join table Devices from the workspace test2

You may have different workspaces containing different kind of data like:
- A workspace for modern workplace stuff
- A workspace for cyber security team stuff
- A workspace for windows update data

To build a perfect dashboard, it can be useful to join data from a workspace to another one.

With KQL it's possible to join data from a workspace to another using the **workspace** expression which allows you to query data across Log Analytics workspaces.

It works as below:

```
workspace("YourWorkspace").Table1
```

In the above query, we need to join table Table1 from the workspace YourWorkspace.

Here we have two workspaces: test1 and test2.
We are working on the test1 workspace and need to access to some data from the devices table located in the workspace test2.

The KQL query for our example is:

```
workspace("test2").Devices
```

4. Join table Devices from test2 on the DeviceName property

As mentioned, just above, to query data from a specific workspace we must use the workspace expression.

```
workspace("YourWorkspace").Table
```

Now to join a table on a specific property we need to add on, here it's DeviceName so it will be on DeviceName.
See below the query:

```
workspace("test2").Devices on DeviceName
```

5. Display records for Lenovo devices from the last 7 days from the test1 workspace

Here we want to join data from a specific workspace just like before but now we want to filter on a condition.

```
workspace("YourWorkspace").Table
| Your Condition
```

We want to get only last records for each device. As we have seen previously you can do by playing with the **timegenerated** property as below:

```
| summarize arg_max(TimeGenerated,*) by DeviceName
```

See below the KQL query to get last records based on the DeviceName column from the test1 workspace:

```
workspace("test1").Devices
| summarize arg_max(TimeGenerated,*) by DeviceName
| where Manufacturer=="LENOVO"
```

 DAY 29

2. Download the BIOS_lab.json file
   https://github.com/damienvanrobaeys/Learn-KQL-in-one-month/blob/main/ExternalData/BIOS_lab.json

3. Upload the file somewhere like Azure blob storage

Here is an example of link after uploading file to Azure blob storage:
https://storageAccount.blob.core.windows.net/container/BIOS_lab.json

4. Load the data from the uploaded JSON with KQL

Here we want to load data directly from an external source.
In our example we have a list of BIOS update information from devices into a JSON file.
We wan to display content of this file with KQL.
To load data from an external source, the operator to use is **externaldata**.

It works as below:

```
externaldata(Column1:Type,Column2:Type…)
[
h@'Link of the file'
]
with(format='format of the file')
```

format can be csv, multijson, json, txt, raw…

In case of loading data from a CSV file, the ignoreFirstRecord (Boolean) property can be useful. If set to true, the first record in every file is ignored. This property is useful when querying CSV files with headers.

See below more information about format:
https://learn.microsoft.com/en-us/azure/data-explorer/ingestion-supported-formats

In our example the KQL query is:

```
externaldata(ComputerName: string, UserName: string,
DeviceModel: string, NotUpdatedSince: string,
CurrentVersionBIOS: string, NewVersionBIOS: string,
BIOSStatus: string, ScriptStatus: string, DateDiffDelay:
string)
[
h@'
https://storageAccount.blob.core.windows.net/Container/BIOS_
lab.json
'
]
with(format='multijson')
```

5. Use the below JSON link from my GitHub
   https://raw.githubusercontent.com/damienvanrobaeys/Intune
   -Reporting/master/BIOS_lab.json

6. Load data directly from this JSON

Now instead of loading file from a blob storage, we will load data
from a file on GitHub.
Here is the same file than before from my GitHub.

See below the query:

```
externaldata(ComputerName: string, UserName: string,
DeviceModel: string, NotUpdatedSince: string,
CurrentVersionBIOS: string, NewVersionBIOS: string,
BIOSStatus: string, ScriptStatus: string, DateDiffDelay:
string)
[
h@'https://raw.githubusercontent.com/damienvanrobaeys/Learn-
KQL-in-one-month/master/ExternalData/BIOS_lab.json'
]
with(format='multijson')
```

See below the result:

ComputerName	UserName	DeviceModel	NotUpdatedSin...	CurrentVersionBIOS	NewVersionBIOS	BIOSStatus	ScriptStatus	DateDiffDelay
> LP00001	Damien	T14s	0	1.21	1.21	uptodate	Success	0
> LP00002	Kevin	T14s	320	1.15	1.21	notuptodate	Success	180_365
> LP00003	Stephen	T14s	320	1.15	1.21	notuptodate	Success	180_365
> LP00004	Mike	T14s	89	1.19	1.21	notuptodate	Success	1_180
> LP00005	Thomas	T14s	0	1.21	1.21	uptodate	Success	0
> LP00006	Luca	T14s	421	1.13	1.21	notuptodate	Success	365_730
> LP00007	Evrard	T14s	89	1.19	1.21	notuptodate	Success	1_180

 DAY 30

2. Use the below JSON link from my GitHub
https://raw.githubusercontent.com/damienvanrobaeys/Learn-KQL-in-one-month/master/ExternalData/Devices.json
3. Load the data from the JSON with KQL

We will use the **externaldata** operator as below:

```
externaldata(devicename: string, username: string,
manufacturer: string)
[
h@'https://raw.githubusercontent.com/damienvanrobaeys/Learn-
KQL-in-one-month/master/ExternalData/Devices.json'
]
with(format='multijson')
```

See below the result:

devicename	···	username	···	manufacturer
> Computer1		damien.vanrobaeys		lenovo
> Computer2		luca.vanrobaeys		lenovo
> Computer3		walter.white		dell
> Computer4		jessie.pinkman		lenovo
> Computer5		gustavo.fringe		hp
> Computer6		tony.soprano		dell
> Computer7		jax.teller		lenovo

4. Join the previous BSOD table to the external data

The first step to join external data to an existing table is to add the external into a variable, this way we can call it.
We will proceed as below:

```
let Table2=externaldata(Column1: Type, Column2: Type...)
[
h@'File link'
]
with(format='format');
```

Then you can join the existing table as below:

```
Table1
| join Table2 on CommonID
```

See below the full query in our example:

```
let Devices=externaldata(devicename: string, username:
string, manufacturer: string)
[
h@'https://raw.githubusercontent.com/damienvanrobaeys/Learn-
KQL-in-one-month/master/ExternalData/Devices.json'
]
with(format='multijson');
let BSOD=datatable
(devicename:string,BSODCount:int,BSODCode:string,Model:strin
g,BIOSVersion:string)
[
    "Computer1","4","0x000000A0","ThinkPad T480s","1.49",
    "Computer2","1","0x00000116","ThinkPad T14s","1.24 ",
    "Computer3","15","0x000000A0","ThinkPad T14s
Gen2","1.50",
    "Computer4","0","0x00000154","ThinkPad T14s
Gen3","1.50",
];
Devices
| join BSOD on devicename
```

See below the result:

devicename	username	manufacturer	devicename1	BSODCount	BSODCode	Model	BIOSVersion
Computer1	damien.vanrobaeys	lenovo	Computer1	4	0x000000A0	ThinkPad T480s	1.49
Computer2	luca.vanrobaeys	lenovo	Computer2	1	0x00000116	ThinkPad T14s	1.24
Computer3	walter.white	dell	Computer3	15	0x000000A0	ThinkPad T14s Gen2	1.50
Computer4	jessie.pinkman	lenovo	Computer4	0	0x00000154	ThinkPad T14s Gen3	1.50

5. Use the below JSON link from my GitHub
    https://raw.githubusercontent.com/damienvanrobaeys/Learn-
    KQL-in-one-month/master/ExternalData/BSOD.json

6. Load the data from the BSOD JSON with KQL

```
externaldata(devicename: string, BSODCount: int, BSODCode:
string, Model: string, BIOSVersion: string)
[
h@'https://raw.githubusercontent.com/damienvanrobaeys/Learn-
KQL-in-one-month/master/ExternalData/BSOD.json'
]
with(format='multijson')
```

7. Join both data from both JSON files

We need to add two external operators for both JSON files into two variables.
See below the full KQL query:

```
let BSOD=externaldata(devicename: string, BSODCount: int,
BSODCode: string, Model: string, BIOSVersion: string)
[
h@'https://raw.githubusercontent.com/damienvanrobaeys/Learn-
KQL-in-one-month/master/ExternalData/BSOD.json'
]
with(format='multijson');
let Devices=externaldata(devicename: string, username:
string, manufacturer: string)
[
h@'https://raw.githubusercontent.com/damienvanrobaeys/Learn-
KQL-in-one-month/master/ExternalData/Devices.json'
]
with(format='multijson');
Devices
| join BSOD on devicename
```

 DAY 31

2. Decode the following base64 code to a string:

SGVsbG8sIHdlbGNvbWUgaW4gdGhlICJMZWFybiBLUUwgaW4gb25lIG1vbnRoIiBib29rLCAyMDI1IGVkaXRpb24uCkhvcGUgeB5b3Ugd2lsbCBlbmpveSBpdA==

Encoding is a basic threat technic where data are transformed into a specific format to be executed on a device.
It's something common in Windows with PowerShell.
This encoding structure is called base 64.
You can easily encode a text, file, picture to a base 64 format through PowerShell or some website like this one:
https://www.base64encode.org

Decoding base64 can be very useful for threat hunting stuff with KQL. To proceed we will use **base64_decode_tostring** function. This one will decode a base64 structure to a string.

It works as below:

```
base64_decode_tostring(Base64 string to decode)
```

In our exercise, the base64 is the below one:
SGVsbG8sIHdlbGNvbWUgaW4gdGhlICJMZWFybiBLUUwgaW4gb25lIG1vbnRoIiBib29rLCAyMDI1IGVkaXRpb24uCkhvcGUgeB5b3Ugd2lsbCBlbmpveSBpdA==

The first step is to add it in a variable. As we have seen on the day 11, we can do it using the let operator, as below:

```
let b64_string =
'SGVsbG8sIHdlbGNvbWUgaW4gdGhlICJMZWFybiBLUUwgaW4gb25lIG1vbnRoIiBib29rLCAyMDI1IGVkaXRpb24uCkhvcGUgeB5b3Ugd2lsbCBlbmpveSBpdA==';
```

The next step is now the use the base64_decode_tostring function to decode our variable.

See below the full KQL query:

```
let b64_string =
'SGVsbG8sIHdlbGNvbWUgaW4gdGhlICJMZWFybiBLUUwgaW4gb25lIG1vbnR
oIiBib29rLCAyMDI1IGVkaXRpb24uCkhvcGluZyB5b3Ugd2lsbCBlbmpveSB
pdA==';
print base64_decode_tostring(b64_string)
```

See below the result:

Hello, welcome in the "Learn KQL in one month" book, 2025 edition. Hoping you will enjoy it.

3. Now do the opposite and encode the below string to base64:
   Hello, let's encode me to base64

To decode base64 we used the **base64_decode_tostring** function.
To encode a string to base64 the function to use is **base64_encode_tostring**. It works as below:

```
base64_encode_tostring("String to encode")
```

See below the KQL query to encode our string:

```
print base64_encode_tostring("Hello, let's encode me to base64")
```

See below the result:
SGVsbG8sIGxldCdzIGVuY29kZSBtZSB0byBiYXNlNjQ=

Now let's encode it again using the KQL function we have seen before:

```
let encoded_string = base64_encode_tostring("Hello, let's encode me to base64");
print base64_decode_tostring(encoded_string)
Hello, let's encode me to base64
```

4. Geolocate IP address 20.53.203.50

Geolocating information about a specific IP address can be done using the **geo_info_from_ip_address** and works as below:

```
geo_info_from_ip_address(IP to locate)
```

See below the KQL query to get location about the RemoteIP:

```
let IPInfo = geo_info_from_ip_address("20.53.203.50");
```

See below the result:

```
print_0
>    {"country":"Australia","state":"New South Wales","city":"Sydney","latitude":-33.8715,"longitude":151.2006}
```

5. Extract values country, state and city

The **geo_info_from_ip_address** function retrieves the below information: Country, state, city, latitude, longitude.

Now we need to extract only some values from the location in the IPInfo column.
As we have seen on the day 17, we will use the **parse_json** operator.
See below the full KQL query:

```
let IPInfo = geo_info_from_ip_address("20.53.203.50");
let JSON_Content=parse_json(IPInfo);
let country=JSON_Content.country;
let city=JSON_Content.city;
let state=JSON_Content.state;
print country=country, city=city, state=state
```

See below the result:

country	city	state
> Australia	Sydney	New South Wales

Here below is another example to do a geolocation on the remoteip address from the WindowsFirewall table.

```
WindowsFirewall
| extend IPInfo = geo_info_from_ip_address(RemoteIP)
| where IPInfo <> "{}"
| extend JSON_Content=parse_json(IPInfo)
| extend country=JSON_Content.country
| extend city=JSON_Content.city
| extend latitude=JSON_Content.latitude
| extend longitude=JSON_Content.longitude
| project Computer, country, city, latitude, longitude
```

See below the result:

Computer	country	city	latitude	longitude
> SQL00.na.contosohotels.com	United States	Tappahannock	37.9273	-76.8545
> SQL00.na.contosohotels.com	United States	Tappahannock	37.9273	-76.8545
> SQL00.na.contosohotels.com	United States	Tappahannock	37.9273	-76.8545
> SQL00.na.contosohotels.com	United States	Tappahannock	37.9273	-76.8545
> SQL00.na.contosohotels.com	United States	Tappahannock	37.9273	-76.8545
> SQL00.na.contosohotels.com	United States	Tappahannock	37.9273	-76.8545

6. In the WindowsFirewall log, filter on private IP address

Searching for private IP address can be useful for threat hunting stuff.
To detect if a specific address is private or public, the function to use **is ipv4_is_private**.
It is used to detect if a specific ipv4 address belongs to a set of private network Ips.
It works as below:

```
ipv4_is_private(IP to check)
```

Here we want to filter on private IP address in the WindowsFirewall log. We will then proceed as below:

```
WindowsFirewall
| extend IsPrivate = ipv4_is_private(RemoteIP)
| where IsPrivate=="true"
```

7. In the SecurityEvent log, filter on eventid 4688 (a new process has been created), where commandline is powershell and contains encodedcommand

We will use where operator to filter on our need, as below:
- where EventID==4688
- CommandLine contains "powershell"
- CommandLine contains "encoded"

See below the KQL query:

```
SecurityEvent
| where EventID == 4688 and CommandLine contains
"powershell.exe" and CommandLine contains "EncodedCommand"
```

8. Parse commandline to extract the encoded command in a new variable

We have seen how to use the parse operator in the day 17.
We need here to extract content from the commandline column.

This one looks like as below:

"C:\windows\System32\WindowsPowershell\v1.0\powershell.exe" -noninteractive -outputFormat xml -NonInteractive -encodedCommand IABbAEUAbgB2AGkAcgBvAG4AbQBlAG4AdABdADoAOgBPAFMAVg BlAHIAcwBpAG8AbgAuAFYAZQByAHMAaQBvAG4AIAA= -inputFormat xml

We want to get only the value for the encoded command meaning after encodedcommand and before -input.
The appropriate parse query is:

```
| parse CommandLine with * "encodedCommand " encodedCommand
" -input" *
```

See below the full KQL query:

```
SecurityEvent
| where EventID == 4688 and CommandLine contains
"powershell.exe" and CommandLine contains "EncodedCommand"
| parse CommandLine with * "encodedCommand " encodedCommand
"-input" *
| project Computer,encodedCommand
```

See below the result:

Computer	encodedCommand
> DC01.na.contosohotels.com	IABbAEUAbgB2AGkAcgBvAG4AbQBlAG4AdABdADoAOgBPAFMAVgBlAHIAcwBpAG8AbgAuAFYAZQByAHMAaQBvAG4AIAA=
> DC01.na.contosohotels.com	IABbAEUAbgB2AGkAcgBvAG4AbQBlAG4AdABdADoAOgBPAFMAVgBlAHIAcwBpAG8AbgAuAFYAZQByAHMAaQBvAG4AIAA=
> RETAILVM01	IABbAEUAbgB2AGkAcgBvAG4AbQBlAG4AdABdADoAOgBPAFMAVgBlAHIAcwBpAG8AbgAuAFYAZQByAHMAaQBvAG4AIAA=
> RETAILVM01	IABbAEUAbgB2AGkAcgBvAG4AbQBlAG4AdABdADoAOgBPAFMAVgBlAHIAcwBpAG8AbgAuAFYAZQByAHMAaQBvAG4AIAA=
> AppBE00.na.contosohotels.com	IABbAEUAbgB2AGkAcgBvAG4AbQBlAG4AdABdADoAOgBPAFMAVgBlAHIAcwBpAG8AbgAuAFYAZQByAHMAaQBvAG4AIAA=
> AppBE00.na.contosohotels.com	IABbAEUAbgB2AGkAcgBvAG4AbQBlAG4AdABdADoAOgBPAFMAVgBlAHIAcwBpAG8AbgAuAFYAZQByAHMAaQBvAG4AIAA=

9. Decode the encoded command in the new variable from base64 to a string

Now we need to decode from the column we created, encodedcommand.
See below the KQL query for that:

```
| parse CommandLine with * "encodedCommand " encodedCommand
" -input" *
| extend DecodedCommand =
base64_decode_tostring(encodedCommand)
```

See below the full KQL query:

```
SecurityEvent
| where EventID == 4688 and CommandLine contains
"powershell.exe" and CommandLine contains "EncodedCommand"
| parse CommandLine with * "encodedCommand " encodedCommand
" -input" *
| extend DecodedCommand =
base64_decode_tostring(encodedCommand)
| project Computer,DecodedCommand,encodedCommand
```

See below the result:

Results   Chart

Computer	DecodedCommand	encodedCommand
> SQL10.na.contosohotels.com	[Environment]::OSVersion.Version	IABbAEUAbgB2AGkAcgBvAG4AbQBlAG4AdABdADoAOgBPAFMAVgBlAHIAcwBpAG8AbgAuAFYAZQByAHMAaQBvAG4AIAA=
> SQL01.na.contosohotels.com	[Environment]::OSVersion.Version	IABbAEUAbgB2AGkAcgBvAG4AbQBlAG4AdABdADoAOgBPAFMAVgBlAHIAcwBpAG8AbgAuAFYAZQByAHMAaQBvAG4AIAA=
> DC11.na.contosohotels.com	[Environment]::OSVersion.Version	IABbAEUAbgB2AGkAcgBvAG4AbQBlAG4AdABdADoAOgBPAFMAVgBlAHIAcwBpAG8AbgAuAFYAZQByAHMAaQBvAG4AIAA=
> DC11.na.contosohotels.com	[Environment]::OSVersion.Version	IABbAEUAbgB2AGkAcgBvAG4AbQBlAG4AdABdADoAOgBPAFMAVgBlAHIAcwBpAG8AbgAuAFYAZQByAHMAaQBvAG4AIAA=

BONUS

Building your first workbook

About the workbook lab

Why this workbook lab?

In this part we will build a workbook, meaning dashboard, from scratch.
The goal is to understand why KQL can be very useful.

Workbook lab resources

To create the workbook, we will play with data from a CSV file.
We have a CSV containing fake data about BIOS update on devices.

See below content of this CSV:

	A	B	C	D	E	F	G	H
	ComputerName	UserName	DeviceModel	NotUpdatedSince	CurrentVersionBIOS	NewVersionBIOS	BIOSStatus	ScriptStatus
	LP00001	Damien	T14s	0	1.21	1.21	uptodate	Success
	LP00002	Kevin	T14s	320	1.15	1.21	notuptodate	Success
	LP00003	Stephen	T14s	320	1.15	1.21	notuptodate	Success
	LP00004	Christophe	T14s	89	1.19	1.21	notuptodate	Success
	LP00005	Thomas	T14s	0	1.21	1.21	uptodate	Success
	LP00006	Luca	T14s	421	1.13	1.21	notuptodate	Success
	LP00007	Evrard	T14s	89	1.19	1.21	notuptodate	Success
	LP00008	Steven	T14s	0	1.21	1.21	uptodate	Success
	LP00009	Pascal	T14s	421	1.13	1.21	notuptodate	Success
	LP00010	Solenn	T490s	752	1.55	1.73	notuptodate	Success
	LP00011	Jean-Christophe	T490s	456	1.67	1.73	notuptodate	Success
	LP00012	Joël	T490s	456	1.67	1.73	notuptodate	Success
	LP00013	André	X280	390	1.41	1.44	notuptodate	Success
	LP00014	Hervé	X280	0	1.44	1.44	uptodate	Success

The idea here is to send all those data into Log Analytics, in a Custom log.
For the lab I already converted the CSV to a JSON.

Resources for the lab are available on the below link:
https://github.com/damienvanrobaeys/Learn-KQL-in-one-month

See below what contains the lab:
- KQL_Lab.csv: CSV with data to send
- KQL_Lab.json: CSV converted to JSON
- Send_to_LA.ps1: script to send CSV content to Log Analytics

Prerequisites

To create our lab workbook, we will need below things:
- Azure subscription
- Access to Log Analytics
- A Log Analytics workspace
- At least contributor rights on the workspace
- Permissions to create data collection rules in the workspace
- A resource group for the data collection endpoint and DCR

Prepare the lab

To send data to the Log Analytics workspace we need:
- A Microsoft Entra application for API calls
- A data collection endpoint (DCE)
- A data collection rules (DCR)

To send custom data to Log Analytics we need to use the Log Ingestion API with PowerShell and to configure a DCE and a DCR.

The DCE (data collection endpoint) is a connection used by the Logs ingestion API to send data for processing and ingestion into Azure Monitor.

The DCR (Data Collection Rule) is used to send data to a Custom Log.
DCRs specify for instance what data should be collected, how to transform that data, and where to send it.
When we create the DCR we need to specify the structure of the table from a JSON file.

Both DCE and DCE should be in same region as Log Analytics workspace, to receive data.

Create the App registration

In this part will create an app registration that will be used to authenticate and send API calls to Log Analytics to send data.

For that we will proceed as below:
1. Go to the Entra portal

2. Go to **App registration**
3. Click on **New registration**
4. Type a name
5. Let by default
6. Click on **Register**
7. Once created, go to **Overview**
8. Copy Application (client) ID
9. Go to **Certificates & secrets**
10. Go to **Client secrets**
11. Click on **New client secret**
12. Type a name
13. Choose a delay
14. Click on **Add**
15. Once created, copy the secret

Prepare the data

The first step is to prepare the table to receive the data.
We need to prepare the structure of the log.
For that we will export content of the CSV to a JSON file.
In the resources for the book, I already uploaded the JSON file.
The JSON file to use is: **KQL_lab.json**

Create data collection endpoint

1. Go to the Entra portal
2. Go to **Monitor**
3. Go to **Data Collection Endpoints**
4. Click on **Create**
5. Type **KQLLab**
6. Choose a subscription
7. Choose a resource group or create a new one
8. Choose a region
9. The region should be the same than the workspace
10. Click on **Review+Create** then **Create**
11. Once created, click on **KQLLab**
12. Go to **overview**
13. Copy the Logs Ingestion value

Create custom log (DCR)

Here we will create a new table based on a DCR.
The DCR (Data Collection Rule) is used to send data to this table.
DCRs specify for instance what data should be collected, how to transform that data, and where to send it.
When we create the DCR we need to specify the structure of the table from a JSON file.

We will proceed as below:
1. Go to your Log Analytics workspaces
2. Go to **Tables**
3. Click on **Create**
4. Click on **New custom log (DCR based)**
5. Type **KQLLab**
6. Click on **Create a new data collection rule**
7. Choose the Subscription,
8. Choose a Resource group
9. Type **KQLLab**
10. Select the DCR **KQLLab**
11. Click on **Next**
12. Click on **Browse for files**
13. Select the **KQL_Lab.json** file
14. Click on **Next**
15. Once created, go to **Monitor**
16. Go to **Data collection rules**
17. Go to **KQLLab**
18. Go to **Overview**
19. Click on **JSON View**
20. Copy the **immutableId** value

Now we have the new table, our new Custom Log that will contain custom data we need to send.
You can see the structure of new table as below:
1. Go to **Tables**
2. Click on the new table
3. Click on the **...**
4. Click **Edit schema**
5. You can see the columns added

Now we need to give the application permission to use the DCR.
For that proceed as below:
1. Go to the DCR **KQL_Lab**
2. Go to **Access Control (IAM)**

207

3. Click on **Add role assignment**.
4. Check **Monitoring Metrics Publisher**
5. Click on **Next**
6. Check **User, group, or service principal**
7. Click on **Select members**
8. Search the app registration
9. Click on **Select**
10. Click on **Review + assign**

Send data to Log Analytics

To send data from the CSV to the workspace we will proceed as below:
1. Use the script: **Send_to_LA.ps1**
2. Edit the script
3. Fill the below variables
   - $tenantId = <your entra app tenant id>
   - $appId = <your entra app client id>
   - $appSecret = <your entra app secret>
   - $DcrImmutableId = <available in DCR, JSON view>
   - $DceURI = <available in DCE, Logs Ingestion value
   - $Table = "KQL_Lab_CL" # custom log to create
4. Run the script
5. Now if you go to your Log Analytics workspace > Logs > Custom log, the new log should be available

So far, we have created the lab, now let's build a workbook using data from the new log.

Building the workbook

What do we want?
First step is to specify what we want to display, which data, which kind of charts...

BIOS update details (uptodate and not uptodate)
We want to display results exactly like in the CSV.
Data should be displayed in a table (in a Grid).

Top 10 devices with old BIOS
We want to display here the top 10 devices with older BIOS version.
Data should be displayed in a table (in a Grid).

Devices with BIOS > 2 years
We want to display devices with BIOS version older than 2 years.
Data should be displayed in a table (in a Grid).

BIOS update status
We want to display:
- Number of devices with BIOS UpToDate
- Number of devices with BIOS not UpToDate
- Data should be displayed in Pie chart

Devices with BIOS not uptodate (per model)
We want to display number of devices with BIOS not up to date by models.
Data should be displayed in Pie chart.

Create the workbook

To create the workbook, proceed as below:
1. Go to your workspace
2. Go to **Workbooks**
3. Click on **New**
4. On the existing query click on Remove > Yes

Adding queries

Top 10 devices with old BIOS
The query should answer to the following criteria:
- Top 10 devices with old BIOS
- We want the last records for each device
- BIOS status should ne notuptodate
- Data should be displayed in a table

See below the KQL query to use:

```
BIOSLab_CL
| summarize arg_max(TimeGenerated,*) by ComputerName
| where BIOSStatus == "notuptodate"
| top 10 by NotUpdatedSince desc nulls last
| project
Device=ComputerName,User=UserName,Model=DeviceModel,['Not
updated since (in days']=NotUpdatedSince,['Current BIOS
version']=CurrentVersionBIOS,['New BIOS
version']=NewVersionBIOS,BIOSStatus,DateDiffDelay
```

Now to add the query proceed as below:
1. In the workbook, click on **Add** > **Add query**

+ Add ⌄

💬 Add text

</> Add parameters

☰ Add links/tabs

⊞ Add query

2. Type above query in **Log Analytics workspace Logs Query**

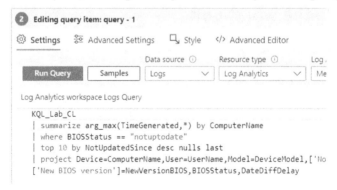

3. Click on **Run query**
4. Click on **Done editing**

5. See below the first overview

6. Click on **Edit** on the query

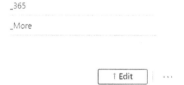

7. Go to **Size** and choose **Small**

8. Go to **Advanced settings**

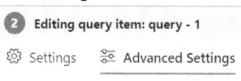

9. In **Chart title** type: Top 10 devices with old BIOS
10. Go to **Style**

11. Check **Show border around content**

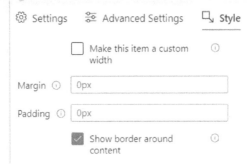

12. Click on **Done editing**
13. Now the design is a bit better

Top 10 devices with old BIOS

Device ↑↓	User ↑↓	Model ↑↓	Not updated since (in days) ↑↓	Current BIOS version ↑↓	New BIOS version ↑↓	BIOSStatus ↑↓	DateDiffDelay ↑↓
LP00004	Mike	T14s	89	1.10	1.21	notuptodate	1_180
LP00007	Evrard	T14s	89	1.19	1.21	notuptodate	1_160
LP00036	Rudy	T460s	703	1.47	1.53	notuptodate	365_730
LP00039	Medhi	X260	609	1.43	1.47	notuptodate	365_730
LP00006	Luca	T14s	421	1.13	1.21	notuptodate	365_730
LP00009	Pascal	T14s	421	1.13	1.21	notuptodate	365_730

Devices with BIOS > 2 years

The query should answer to the following criteria:

- BIOS date > 730 days (DateDiffDelay = 730_More)
- We want the last records for each device
- BIOS status should be notuptodate
- Data should be displayed in a table

See below the KQL query to use:

```
KQL_Lab_CL
| summarize arg_max(TimeGenerated,*) by ComputerName
| where BIOSStatus == "notuptodate"
| where DateDiffDelay == "730_More"
| project
Device=ComputerName,User=UserName,Model=DeviceModel,['Not
updated since (in days']=NotUpdatedSince,['Current BIOS
version']=CurrentVersionBIOS,['New BIOS
version']=NewVersionBIOS,BIOSStatus,DateDiffDelay
```

Now to add the query proceed as below:
1. In the workbook, click on **Add > Add query**
2. Type above query in **Log Analytics workspace Logs Query**

3. Click on **Run query**
4. Click on **Done editing**
5. Go to **Size** and choose **Small**
6. Go to **Advanced settings**
7. In **Chart title** type: Devices with BIOS > 2 years
8. Go to **Style**
9. Check **Show border around content**
10. Click on **Done editing**
11. See below an overview:

Devices with BIOS > 2 years

Device ↑↓	User ↑↓	Model ↑↓	Not updated since (in days ↑↓	Current BIOS version ↑↓	New BIOS version ↑↓	BIOSStatus ↑↓	DateDiffDelay ↑↓
LP00033	Harjit	T470s	1379	1.17	1.41	notuptodate	730_More
LP00034	Octavio	T470s	1110	1.27	1.41	notuptodate	730_More
LP00035	Mattias	T460s	1907	1.15	1.53	notuptodate	730_More
LP00037	Angel	T460s	2023	1.11	1.53	notuptodate	730_More
LP00040	Bruce	X260	1580	1.21	1.47	notuptodate	730_More

BIOS update details (uptodate and not uptodate)

The query should answer to the following criteria:
- We want the last records for each device
- All BIOS status uptodate and notuptodate
- Data should be displayed in a table

See below the KQL query to use:

```
KQL_Lab_CL
| summarize arg_max(TimeGenerated,*) by ComputerName
| project
Device=ComputerName,User=UserName,Model=DeviceModel,['Not
updated since (in days']=NotUpdatedSince,['Current BIOS
version']=CurrentVersionBIOS,['New BIOS
version']=NewVersionBIOS,BIOSStatus,DateDiffDelay
```

Now to add the query proceed as below:
1. In the workbook, click on **Add** > **Add query**
2. Type above query in **Log Analytics workspace Logs Query**
3. Click on **Run query**
4. Click on **Done editing**
5. Go to **Size** and choose **Small**
6. Go to **Advanced settings**
7. In **Chart title** type:
8. Go to **Style**
9. Check **Show border around content**
10. Click on **Done editing**

11. See below an overview:

BIOS update details (uptodate and not uptodate)

Device	User	Model	Not updated since (in days)	Current BIOS version	New BIOS version	BIOSStatus	DateDiffDelay
LP00001	Damien	T14s	0	1.21	1.21	uptodate	0
LP00002	Kevin	T14s	320	1.15	1.21	notuptodate	180_365
LP00003	Stephen	T14s	320	1.15	1.21	notuptodate	180_365
LP00004	Mike	T14s	89	1.19	1.21	notuptodate	1_180
LP00005	Thomas	T14s	0	1.21	1.21	uptodate	0
LP00006	Luca	T14s	421	1.13	1.21	notuptodate	365_730

BIOS Update status

The query should answer to the following criteria:
- We want the last records for each device
- BIOS status uptodate and notuptodate
- Count number of devices uptodate and notuptodate
- Data should be displayed in a Pie chart

See below the KQL query to use:

```
KQL_Lab_CL
| where ScriptStatus == "Success"
| summarize arg_max(TimeGenerated,*) by ComputerName
| summarize BIOSLab_CL = count() by BIOSStatus
```

Now to add the query proceed as below:
1. In the workbook, click on **Add > Add query**
2. Type above query in **Log Analytics workspace Logs Query**
3. Click on **Run query**
4. Click on **Done editing**
5. Go to **Size** and choose **Small**
6. Go to **Visualization** and select **Pie chart**
7. Go to A**dvanced settings**
8. In **Chart title** type: BIOS update status
9. Go to **Style**
10. Check **Show border around content**
11. Click on **Done editing**
12. See below an overview:

BIOS update status

uptodate	notuptodate	uptodate
3	6	1

notuptodate	notuptodate	
1	2	1

Devices with BIOS not uptodate (per model)

The query should answer to the following criteria:
- We want the last records for each device
- BIOS status should ne notuptodate
- Data should be displayed in a chart

See below the KQL query to use:

```
KQL_Lab_CL
| summarize arg_max(TimeGenerated,*) by ComputerName
| where BIOSStatus == "notuptodate"
| summarize BIOSLab_CL = count() by DeviceModel
```

Now to add the query proceed as below:
1. In the workbook, click on **Add** > **Add query**
2. Type above query in **Log Analytics workspace Logs Query**
3. Click on **Run query**
4. Click on **Done editing**
5. Go to **Size** and choose **Small**
6. Go to **Advanced settings**
7. In **Chart title** type: Devices model with BIOS not uptodate
8. Go to **Style**
9. Check **Show border around content**
10. Click on **Done editing**
11. See below an overview:

Devices with BIOS not uptodate (per model)

T14s	T470s	T460s	T450s	X260
6	2	3	1	2

Adding tab

In the workbook, we have two kinds of data:
- Table
- Chart

Now we want to display each kind of data in a specific tab:
- Overview tab with data in table
- Details tab with data in chart

To do this we will add two tabs as below:
1. Click on **Add** > **Add links/tabs**

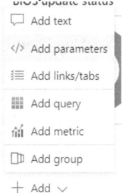

2. In **Style**, choose **Tabs**

3. Configure as below:
   - Tab name: Overview and Details
   - Action: Set a parameter value for both
   - Value: SelectedTab
   - Settings: Overview and Details
4. See below:

5. Click on **Done editing**
6. On the new tab click on **Edit** > **Move** > **Move to top**
7. Then click on Move down
8. We now have two tabs but need to bind queries to them

9. On each query, click on **Edit**
10. Go to **Advanced settings**

11. Check **Make this item conditionnaly visible**

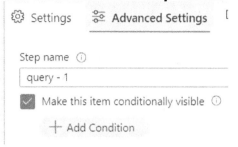

12. Click on **Add condition**
13. In **Parameter name**, type **SelectedTab**
14. Choose **equals**
15. In **Parameter value**, type **Overview** or **Details** depending of the query type

Now the Overview tab will contain only chart

The Details tab will contain only table

Overview   Details

Top 10 devices with old BIOS

Device ↑↓	User ↑↓	Model ↑↓	Not updated since (in days ↑↓	Current BIOS version ↑↓	New BIOS version ↑↓	E
LP00004	Mike	T14s	89	1.19	1.21	r
LP00007	Evrard	T14s	89	1.19	1.21	r
LP00036	Rudy	T460s	703	1.47	1.53	r
LP00039	Medhi	X260	609	1.43	1.47	r
LP00006	Luca	T14s	421	1.13	1.21	r
LP00009	Pascal	T14s	421	1.13	1.21	r

BIOS update details (uptodate and not uptodate)

Device ↑↓	User ↑↓	Model ↑↓	Not updated since (in days ↑↓	Current BIOS version ↑↓	New BIOS version ↑↓	E
LP00001	Damien	T14s	0	1.21	1.21	ᶜ
LP00002	Kevin	T14s	320	1.15	1.21	r
LP00003	Stephen	T14s	320	1.15	1.21	r
LP00004	Mike	T14s	89	1.19	1.21	r

Adding filters

Now we want to add filters to help people to search things on the dashboard.
We want:
- Search bar above table
- A main search to filter on device name in all tables
- A dropdown menu to filter on models

Search bar above table
For that we will do the following actions on each query with table:
1. Click on **Edit**
2. Click on **Advanced settings**
3. Check **Show filter field above grid or tiles**

☑ Show filter field above grid or tiles ⓘ

4. It will display a search bar above the grid

Top 10 devices with old BIOS

🔍 Search			
Device ↑↓	User ↑↓	Model ↑↓	Not u
LP00004	Mike	T14s	89
LP00007	Evrard	T14s	89

Main filter on device name in all tables

We will proceed as below:

1. Go to **Add** > **Add parameters**

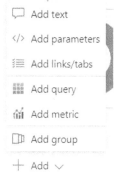

2. Choose **Pills**
3. Click on **Add parameter**

4. In **Parameter name**, type **ComputerName**
5. In **Display name**, type **filter on device name**
6. In **Parameter type**, choose **Text**

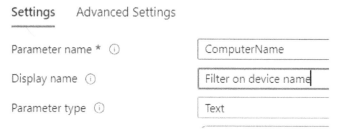

7. Click on **Save**
8. Click on **Done editing**
9. Move the parameter below the tabs
10. Go to each query with table
11. Click on **Edit**
12. Go to **Settings**

13. In the query, add the following line:

```
| where "{ComputerName:escape}" == "*" or ComputerName
contains "{ComputerName:escape}" or "{ComputerName:escape}"
== "All devices"
```

Dropdown menu to filter on models
We will proceed as below:
1. Click on **Edit** on the previous parameter
2. Choose **Pills**
3. Click on **Add parameter**
4. In **Parameter name**, type **Models**
5. In **Display name**, type **filter on models**
6. In **Parameter type**, choose **Drop down**
7. Check **Allow multiple**
8. Go to **Log Analytics workspace Logs query**
9. Type the following query:

```
KQL_Lab_CL
| where ScriptStatus == "Success"
| where DeviceModel <> ""
| distinct DeviceModel
```

10. In **Include in the drop down**, check **All**

11. In **Default selected item**, check **All**

Default selected item ⓘ

| All |

12. Click on **Save**
13. Click on **Done editing**
14. Move the parameter below the tabs
15. Go to each query with table
16. Click on **Edit**
17. Go to **Settings**
18. Add the following line to the query

```
| where DeviceModel_s has_any ({Models})
```

See below the new drop-down menu filter:

Import the workbook

Here instead of creating the workbook step by step, we will import the workbook by importing it from a JSON file.
It can be useful if you find an existing dashboard on the web and want to test/use it in your environment.

The first step is to get the workbook content, available on the below link:

https://github.com/damienvanrobaeys/Learn-KQL-in-one-month/blob/main/Workbook%20lab/Workbook.json

Then we will proceed as below:
1. Go to the Azure portal
2. Go to **Log Analytics workspace**
3. Go to **workbooks**
4. Click on **New**
5. Go to **Advanced editor**
6. Remove all content
7. Go to the GitHub link
8. Click on the copy button
9. Click on **Apply**
10. Click on **Done editing** then **Save**

www.ingramcontent.com/pod-product-compliance
Lightning Source LLC
LaVergne TN
LVHW051228050326
832903LV00028B/2285